D0460097

"Jesus has now long since escaped the confines of church, Christianity, and even religion. book thoughtfully presents a Jesus who is paradoxically both closer to the original and more available to postmodern people than the stained-glass version. The book is bound to provoke both admiration and condemnation which, come to think of it, the maverick Galilean rabbi also did."

—Harvey Cox, Hollis Professor of Divinity at Harvard
and author of *When Jesus Came to Harvard*

"Chopra's book *The Third Jesus* reminds me of the theological work of one of history's greatest humanitarians and the 1952 Nobel Peace Prize Laureate, Dr. Albert Schweitzer. Schweitzer wrote extensively about Jesus and challenged much of the prevailing theology regarding Jesus's life and ideas. Chopra is Schweitzer's equal in bringing to light a fresh and profound way to experience the teachings of Jesus." —David T. Ives, executive director of the
Albert Schweitzer Institute at Quinnipiac University

"In this book, a man shaped by the religions of the East introduces the West to a Jesus we have either lost or have never known. That is itself a stunning concept, but Deepak Chopra is a stunning man. He explores what he calls the 'Christ-consciousness,' which can be identified neither with the Jesus of history nor with the Jesus of the creeds, the doctrines, and the dogmas of the ecclesiastical institution. This 'third Jesus' can be seen only when we move into a new human awareness that will carry us beyond tribe and prejudice and even beyond our religious systems. As a Christian, I welcome his insights into my Jesus and his provocative call to me to enter the Christ-consciousness and thus to become more deeply and completely human."

—John Shelby Spong, retired bishop of the Episcopal Diocese of Newark
and author of *Jesus for the Non-Religious*

"The message of Jesus was clear, simple, and direct. But within a generation of his passion, it was compromised in order to accommodate the widely conflicting views among those who claimed to follow him. In Deepak Chopra's new book, you will find much thought-provoking material related to this compromise, which will elucidate many sensitive issues that have perplexed believers for centuries. In contrast to a message originally intended to inspire people to the wonders of a world reborn in God, the emphasis nowadays makes it almost impossible to think of Jesus or even Christianity itself except in terms of the suffering savior who died to appease God's anger against us. The terrible toll this emphasis has exacted on the message is sensitively treated in a most compelling way in this very valuable new work."

—Miceal Ledwith, L.Ph., L.D., D.D., LL.D, former president and
professor of theology, Maynooth University; served as a member of the
Vatican's International Theological Commission for seventeen years under
Pope John Paul II when Cardinal Joseph Alois Ratzinger was president

"The story of the third Jesus is based on the science of all great religions. The knowledge that God dwells within each of us is realized when we enter into Christ-consciousness. It's critical that great teachers of faith restate the obvious in ways that can be digested by masses. Specifically, that the idea of Nirvana, Samadhi, or Christ-consciousness is found when we become one with the universe. Deepak is one of those great teachers. His voice reaffirms the science that is the basis of all religions and echoes the truth in the human spirit. ॐ "

—Russell Simmons, chairman of Rush Communications

"What happens with an 'outsider' looks at some of the deep teachings of Jesus? Different angles and perspectives are awakened and different questions are asked of the Christ tradition. In this way, wisdom flows in two directions: East to West and West to East, and we all wake up—which is, after all, the purpose of a man and life like Jesus. This book helps to heal the divorce between East and West, underscoring that there is only one wisdom and that it demands much of all of us no matter what tradition we come from and especially at this perilous time in human and earth history when we are finally realizing we are all in this together, and together we will perish or rise."

—Dr. Matthew Fox, author of *One River, Many Wells: Wisdom Springing from Global Faiths; A New Reformation; Original Blessing;* and *The A.W.E. Project: Reinventing Education, Reinventing the Human*

"In this intriguing study of the sayings of Jesus, Deepak Chopra gently releases this highly evolved spiritual teacher, light of the world, and son of God from the limitations of dogmatic theology. With profound wisdom and clarity, Deepak offers the amazing suggestion that the same God-consciousness embodied in the human Jesus is present in all of us individually and collectively. In a spirit of humble knowingness, Deepak encourages us to look deep into the mirror of our collective souls and ponder the question Jesus continues to ask: 'Who do YOU say that I AM?'"

—Sister Judian Breitenbach, Catholic order of the Poor Handmaids of Jesus Christ, founder of the Sari Asher Namasté Center in LaPorte, Indiana

"In this book, Deepak Chopra proposes a Copernican revolution in our understanding of Christianity by replacing the theological version of the holy trinity with the triptych of Jesus as possessing a human, an institutional, and a mystical dimension. By emphasizing the mystical dimension and identifying Jesus as a spiritual revolutionary, he invites Christianity to perform yet another miracle in his name—that of transforming the world once again."

—Arvind Sharma, Birks Professor of Comparative Religion, McGill University

"The hardest thing to see is what is hidden in plain sight. After twenty centuries of doctrine and dogma we have nearly lost sight of the Jesus who was a wandering teacher of mystical truths. In his imaginative reconstruction of the inner meaning of the gospels, Deepak Chopra reminds us of the third Jesus, the enlightened master of God-consciousness. It will disturb the minds of the orthodox, and delight the spirits of mystics and progressive Christians."

—Sam Keen, philosopher and author of *Sightings: Extraordinary Encounters with Ordinary Birds*

"Literate, mainstream Christians will welcome Chopra's championing before the world, the meaning of their commitment to action, practice, 'ortho-praxis,' following the only absolutely unambiguous demands of Jesus on his followers recorded in the New Testament: serving the poor, loving neighbor and even enemies. It is the most effective response to the Dawkins crowd who never even mention the Bishop Robinsons, Martin Luther Kings, Dietrich Bonhoeffers, and Mother Teresas, who, by their actions, have shown their faith in this Jesus Christ."

—Rustum Roy, Evan Pugh Professor Emeritus of the Solid State, professor emeritus of science technology and society, Pennsylvania State University

The Lords of the Light

On the Shores of Eternity

How to Know God

The Soul in Love

The Chopra Center Herbal Handbook
(with coauthor David Simon)

Grow Younger, Live Longer
(with coauthor David Simon)

The Deeper Wound

The Chopra Center Cookbook
(coauthored by David Simon and Leanne Backer)

The Angel Is Near

The Daughters of Joy

Golf for Enlightenment

Soulmate

The Spontaneous Fulfillment of Desire

Peace Is the Way

The Book of Secrets

Fire in the Heart

The Seven Spiritual Laws of Yoga
(with coauthor David Simon)

Magical Beginnings, Enchanted Lives
(coauthored by David Simon and Vicki Abrams)

Life After Death

Buddha

The Essential How to Know God

The Essential Spontaneous Fulfillment of Desire

The Essential Ageless Body, Timeless Mind

DEEPAK CHOPRA

THE

THIRD

JESUS

*How to Find Truth and Love in
Today's World*

RIDER

LONDON · SYDNEY · AUCKLAND · JOHANNESBURG

1 3 5 7 9 10 8 6 4 2

Published in the UK in 2008 by Rider, an imprint of Ebury Publishing

First published in the USA by Harmony Books, an imprint of the Crown
Publishing Group, a division of Random House, Inc., in 2008

Ebury Publishing is a Random House Group company

Copyright © Deepak Chopra 2008

Deepak Chopra has asserted his right to be identified as the author of this
Work in accordance with the Copyright, Designs and Patents Act 1988.

The Random House Group Limited Reg. No. 954009

Addresses for companies within the Random House Group can be found at
www.rbooks.co.uk

A CIP catalogue record for this book is available from the British Library

The Random House Group Limited supports The Forest Stewardship
Council (FSC), the leading international forest certification organisation.
All our titles that are printed on Greenpeace approved FSC certified paper
carry the FSC logo. Our paper procurement policy can be found at
www.rbooks.co.uk/environment

Mixed Sources
Product group from well-managed
forests and other controlled sources
www.fsc.org Cert no. TF-COC-2139
© 1996 Forest Stewardship Council
FSC

Printed in the UK by CPI Mackays, Chatham, ME5 8TD

ISBN 9781846041112

Copies are available at special rates for bulk orders. Contact the sales
development team on 020 7840 8487 or for more information.

To buy books by your favourite authors and register for offers, visit
www.rbooks.co.uk

To the Irish Christian Brothers in India

who introduced me to Jesus when I was a little boy

CONTENTS

CONTENTS

THE

THIRD

JESUS

INTRODUCTION

Jesus Christ left behind a riddle that two thousand years of worship haven't solved. The riddle can be stated in one sentence: Why are Jesus's teachings impossible to live by? It would startle millions of Christians to hear that this riddle exists. They try to live by Jesus's words every day. They love, pray, show compassion, and practice charity in his name. Yet these humane and worthy actions, which reveal a good heart intent on serving God, do not fulfill Jesus's deeper mandate.

What Jesus actually taught is much more radical and at the same time mystical. When I was a child in India, I first heard about the Golden Rule from the Christian brothers who had traveled from Ireland to run our school. This basic tenet of Christianity, which comes from Matthew 7:12, is simple enough to teach even to small children: Do unto others as you would have them do unto you. So where is the riddle? What could possibly be considered radical or mystical here?

Taken literally, the Golden Rule requires you to treat an enemy as an equal, which means in essence that you can have no enemies.

Jesus didn't say, "Pick the easiest people and treat them nicely, just as you'd like to be treated." That might be the Gilded Rule, which is what the Golden Rule became once people realized that Jesus's teaching couldn't be reconciled with human nature. It's human nature to love those who love us in return, not those who hate us. It's human nature to fight back when attacked (this violates another basic but impossible tenet of Jesus's: Resist not evil). But Jesus makes no such allowances. Many of Jesus's most famous words defy human nature in this way. Turn the other cheek. Love thy neighbor as thyself.

If Jesus's words are too radical to live by, was that his intention? Or have we misunderstood a spiritual teacher who seems to be so clear, simple, and direct? I propose that both have occurred. Jesus intended a completely new view of human nature, and unless you transform yourself, you misunderstand what he had to say. You can struggle your entire life to be a good Christian without succeeding in doing what Jesus explicitly wanted.

He wanted to inspire a world reborn in God. This vision is breathtaking in its ambition. It points us toward a mystical realm, the only place where human nature can radically change. At the level of the soul we find out how to love our neighbors as ourselves, we are able to remove the obstacles that keep us from doing unto others as we would want them to do unto us. Jesus's name for the realm of the soul is the Kingdom of God, and he clearly intended for it to descend to earth. (On earth let it be as it is in Heaven.) God was to replace Caesar as the ruler of human affairs, and all the conditions that applied to material existence would change. Jesus could not have been more direct when he said that total transformation was near. This was perhaps the first and most important message he wanted to deliver: From the time Jesus began to preach, he said, "Repent, for the Kingdom of Heaven is at hand." (Matthew 4:17)

Yet Jesus failed to bring about God's rule on earth, and his radical vision became compromised only a generation after his death, at the same time that early Christianity was spreading with startling speed and intensity. The disciples who had followed him knew without a doubt that they had met someone of earthshaking significance. What the disciples didn't talk about so fervently was the shadow side of their new faith. They were struggling to live as Jesus wanted them to, and in many respects they were failing. They fought for power among themselves and squabbled over doctrine. They had doubts, and fears of persecution. Jealousy and sexual desire made their age-old claims. Such basic matters as whether to follow Peter or Paul as chief spokesman for Jesus drove Christians apart.

The early Church was rife with disputes and conflicts, just like every other faith that had come before. To emerge from this chaos, to survive as followers of the Messiah, was a life-and-death challenge. As a result, Christianity was forced to compromise Jesus's vision: The alternative—a complete transformation of human nature—was proving impossible. Those few who could achieve it became known as saints, and they were far removed from the dirty, bustling world and its corrupt ways.

In this book, I argue that Jesus's vision isn't impossible to realize. Yes, it is radical and mystical. None of that has changed. But the underlying dilemma—how to live as Jesus wanted us to—can be resolved. In fact, it must be resolved if Jesus is to have any kind of meaningful future. In order to find the answer to the Jesus riddle, we must begin with radical surgery, cutting through the timeworn Jesus that all of us know (even those, like me, who were not raised in the Church). That traditional version of Jesus was constructed as a compromise; it accepts the essential failure of Christ's vision, so we must go beyond it.

Jesus did not physically descend from God's dwelling place above the clouds, nor did he return to sit at the right hand of a literal throne. What made Jesus the Son of God was the fact that he had achieved God-consciousness. Jesus said as much, over and over, when he declared that "the Father and I are one." He knew no separation between his thoughts and God's thoughts, his feelings and God's feelings, his actions and the actions God wanted performed. I realize that I am quoting the most basic of Jesus's words, but we have no choice but to start at the beginning. "Radical" comes from the Latin word *radix,* or "root." Jesus the radical went to the root of the human condition, and his approach to suffering was to eradicate it, literally to tear it out by the root.

But my attachment to Jesus is more personal, too. It dates from my childhood, when I heard Christian prayers at the Catholic school I attended and Vedic chants at home. I was encouraged to respect every faith, which wasn't a sterile duty but more like a festive delight. In my circle of friends one could run over to a Christian house for Christmas without feeling strange, just as we ran to a Muslim or Parsi house for their feasts and holy observances. I grew up in the early Fifties, and it would be naive to call that an innocent time in India. Hundreds of thousands of Hindus and Muslims suffered and died in the partition of India and Pakistan after liberation from the British in 1947. As one of India's "children of midnight" (so called because the modern nation of India was born at the stroke of midnight, August 15, 1947), I lived on the cusp between idealism and violence.

Now, sixty years later, the world is changing again, rapidly and with tremendous confusion. In the ferment of change there resides an opening for Jesus's radical vision to be renewed. Spirit, like water, remains fresh only if it flows.

I have written what I think the New Testament actually means, astonishing things stated in plain words. No one is an outsider who wishes to make Jesus central to his or her spiritual path, and no one should pay lip service to Jesus's words while guilt, pain, and suffering continue to go unhealed.

Part One

❖

THE THIRD JESUS

REDEEMING THE REDEEMER

Jesus is in trouble. When people worship him today—or even speak his name—the object of their devotion is unlikely to be who they think he is. A mythical Jesus has grown up over time. He has served to divide peoples and nations. He has led to destructive wars in the name of religious fantasies. The legacy of love found in the New Testament has been tainted with the worst sort of intolerance and prejudice that would have appalled Jesus in life. Most troubling of all, his teachings have been hijacked by people who hate in the name of love.

"Sometimes I feel this social pressure to return to my faith," a lapsed Catholic told me recently, "but I'm too bitter. Can I love a religion that calls gays sinners but hides pedophiles in its clergy? Yesterday while I was driving to work, I heard a rock song that went, 'Jesus walked on water when he should have surfed,' and you know what? I burst out laughing. I would never have done that when I was younger. Now I feel only the smallest twinge of guilt."

No matter where you look, a cloud of confusion hangs over the message of Jesus. To cut through it we have to be specific about who we mean when we refer to Jesus. One Jesus is historical, and we know next to nothing about him. Another Jesus is the one appropriated by Christianity. He was created by the Church to fulfill its agenda. The third Jesus, the one this book is about, is as yet so unknown that even the most devout Christians don't suspect that he exists. Yet he is the Christ we cannot—and must not—ignore.

The first Jesus was a rabbi who wandered the shores of northern Galilee many centuries ago. This Jesus still feels close enough to touch. He appears in our mind's eye dressed in homespun but haloed in glory. He was kind, serene, peaceful, loving, and yet he was the keeper of deep mysteries.

This historical Jesus has been lost, however, swept away by history. He still lingers like a ghost, a projection of all the ideal qualities we wish for in ourselves but so painfully lack. Why couldn't there be one person who was perfectly loving, perfectly compassionate, and perfectly humble? There can be if we call him Jesus and remove him to a time thousands of years in the past. (If you live in the East, his name might be Buddha, but the man is equally mythical and equally a projection of our own lack.)

The first Jesus is less than consistent, as a closer reading of the gospels will show. If Jesus was perfectly peaceful, why did he declare, "Do not suppose that I have come to bring peace to the earth. I did not come to bring peace, but a sword"? (Matthew 10:34) If he was perfectly loving, why did he say, "Throw out the unprofitable servant into the outer darkness, where there will be weeping and gnashing of teeth"? (Matthew 25:30) (Sometimes the translation is even harsher, and Jesus commands "the worthless slave" to be consigned to hell.) If Jesus was humble, why did he claim to rule the earth beyond the power of any king? At the very least, the living Jesus was a man of baffling contradictions.

And yet the more contradictions we unearth, the less mythical this Jesus becomes. The flesh-and-blood man who is lost to history must have been extraordinarily human. To be divine, one must be rich in every human quality first. As one famous Indian spiritual teacher once said, "The measure of enlightenment is how comfortable you feel with your own contradictions."

Millions of people worship another Jesus, however, who never existed, who doesn't even lay claim to the fleeting substance of the first Jesus. This is the Jesus built up over thousands of years by theologians and other scholars. He is the Holy Ghost, the Three-in-One Christ, the source of sacraments and prayers that were unknown to the rabbi Jesus when he walked the earth. He is also the Prince of Peace over whom bloody wars have been fought. This second Jesus cannot be embraced without embracing theology first. Theology shifts with the tide of human affairs. Metaphysics itself is so complex that it contradicts the simplicity of Jesus's words. Would he have argued with learned divines over the meaning of the Eucharist? Would he have espoused a doctrine declaring that babies are damned until they are baptized?

The second Jesus leads us into the wilderness without a clear path out. He became the foundation of a religion that has proliferated into some twenty thousand sects. They argue endlessly over every thread in the garments of a ghost. But can any authority, however exalted, really inform us about what Jesus would have thought? Isn't it a direct contradiction to hold that Jesus was a unique creation—the one and only incarnation of God—while at the same time claiming to be able to read his mind on current events? Yet in his name Christianity pronounces on homosexuality, birth control, and abortion.

These two versions of Jesus—the sketchy historical figure and the abstract theological creation—hold a tragic aspect for me, because I blame them for stealing something precious: the Jesus who taught his followers how to reach God-consciousness. I want to offer the possibility that Jesus was truly, as he proclaimed, a savior. Not *the* savior, not the one and only Son of God. Rather, Jesus embodied the highest level of enlightenment. He spent his brief adult life describing it, teaching it, and passing it on to future generations.

Jesus intended to save the world by showing others the path to God-consciousness.

Such a reading of the New Testament doesn't diminish the first two Jesuses. Rather, they are brought into sharper focus. In place of lost history and complex theology, the third Jesus offers a direct relationship that is personal and present. Our task is to delve into scripture and prove that a map to enlightenment exists there. I think it does, undeniably; indeed, it's the living aspect of the gospels. We aren't talking about faith. Conventional faith is the same as belief in the impossible (such as Jesus walking on water), but there is another faith that gives us the ability to reach into the unknown and achieve transformation.

Jesus spoke of the necessity to believe in him as the road to salvation, but those words were put into his mouth by followers writing decades later. The New Testament is an interpretation of Jesus by people who felt reborn but also left behind. In orthodox Christianity they won't be left behind forever; at the Second Coming Jesus will return to reclaim the faithful. But the Second Coming has had twenty centuries to unfold, with the devout expecting it any day, and still it lies ahead. The idea of the Second Coming has been especially destructive to Jesus's intentions, because it postpones what needs to happen now. The Third Coming—finding God-consciousness through your own efforts—happens in the present. I'm using the term as a metaphor for a shift in consciousness that makes Jesus's teachings totally real and vital.

When Jesus Comes Again

Imagine for a moment that you are one of the poor Jewish farmers, fishermen, or other heavy laborers who have heard about a wandering rabbi who promises Heaven, not to the rich and powerful, but to your kind, society's humblest. On this day—we can surmise that it was hot and dry, with the desert sun beating down from overhead—you climb a hill north of the blue inland lake known as the Sea of Galilee.

At the top of the hill Jesus sits with his closest followers, waiting to preach until enough people have gathered. You wait, too, seeking the shade of the crooked olive trees that dot the parched landscape. Jesus (known to you in Hebrew as Yeshua, a fairly common name) delivers a sermon, and you are deeply struck, to the heart, in fact. He promises that God loves you, a statement he makes directly, without asking you to follow the duties of your sect or to respect the ancient, complex laws of the prophets. Further, he says that God loves you best. In the world to come, you and your kind will get the richest rewards, everything you have been denied in this world.

The words sound idealistic to the point of lunacy—if God loved you so much, why did he saddle you with cruel Roman conquerors? Why did he allow you to be enslaved and forced to toil until the day you die? The priests in Jerusalem have explained this many times: As the son of Adam, your sins have brought you a wretched existence, full of misery and endless toil. But Jesus doesn't mention sin. He expands God's love to unbelievable lengths. Did you really hear him right?

You are the light of the world. Let your light shine before all men.

He compares you to a city set upon a hill that can't be hidden because its lights are so bright. You've never been told anything remotely like this or ever seen yourself this way.

Don't judge others, so that you may not be judged. Before you try to take a mote out of your brother's eye, first remove the log from your own.

Do to others what you would have them do to you. This one rule sums up what the law and the prophets taught.

Ask, and it will be given to you. Seek, and you shall find. Knock, and the door will open.

How can you explain your reaction to this preacher—jumbled feelings of disbelief and hope, suspicion and an aching need to believe? You wanted to run away before he was finished, denying everything you heard. No sane man could walk the streets and judge not the thieves, pickpockets, and whores on every corner. It was absurd to claim that all you had to do, if you needed bread and clothes, was to ask God for them. And yet how beautifully Jesus wove the spell:

> Consider the lilies, how they grow: They neither toil nor spin, but I tell you, not even Solomon in all his glory clothed himself like one of these. Consider the crows, for they neither sow nor reap, they have no storeroom or barn, and yet God feeds them. How much more valuable are you than the birds!

Despite years of hard experience that made a lie of Jesus's promises, you believed them while you were listening. You kept believing them as you walked back down the hill near sunset, and for a few days afterward they haunted you. Until they faded away.

Time hasn't altered this mixture of hope and puzzlement. I had an experience that centers around one of Jesus's most baffling teachings: "Whoever hits you on the cheek, offer him the other also." (Luke 6:29) These are words that our Jewish laborer could have heard that day on the hilltop, but time hasn't altered human nature enough to make this teaching any easier. If I let a bully hit me on one cheek only to turn the other, won't he beat the stuffing out of me? The same holds good, on a larger scale, for a threat like terrorism: If we allow evildoers to strike us without reprisal, won't they continue to do so, over and over?

On the surface my experience only vaguely fits this dilemma. Yet it leads to the heart of Christ's mission. I was in a crowded bookstore promoting a new book when a woman came up to me, saying, "Can I talk to you? I need three hours." She was a compact, forceful person (less politely, a pit bull), but as gently as I could I told her, pointing to the other people crowded around the table, that I didn't have three hours to spare.

A cloud passed over her face. "You have to. I came all the way from Mexico City," she said, insisting that she must have three hours alone with me. I asked if she had called my office in advance, and she had. What did they tell her? That I would be busy all day.

"But I came on my own anyway, because I've heard you say that anything is possible," she said. "If that's true, you should be able to see me."

The PR person in charge of the event was pulling at my elbow, so I told the woman that if she came back later, I might find a few minutes of personal time for her. She became enraged in front of everyone. She released a stream of invective, sparing no four-letter words, and stalked away, muttering darkly that I was a fraud. Later that night the incident wouldn't leave me in peace, so I considered an essential spiritual truth: People mirror back to us the reality of who we are. I sat down and wrote out a list of things I'd noticed about this woman. What had I disliked about her? She was angry, demanding, confrontational, and selfish. Then I called my wife and asked her if I was like that. There was a long silence at the other end of the phone. I was more than a little shaken.

I sat down to face what reality was asking me to face. I found a veneer of annoyance and irritation (after all, wasn't I the innocent victim? hadn't she embarrassed me in front of dozens of people?). Then I called a truce with the negative energies she had stirred up. Vague images of past injuries came to mind, which put me on the right trail. I moved as much of the stagnant energies of hurt as I could.

To put it bluntly, this was a Jesus moment. When he preached, "If anyone strikes you on the cheek, offer him the other also" (Luke 6:29), Jesus wasn't preaching masochism or martyrdom. He was speaking of a quality of consciousness that is known in Sanskrit as *Ahimsa*. The word is usually translated as "harmlessness" or "nonviolence," and in modern times it became the watchword of Gandhi's movement of peaceful resistance. Gandhi himself was often seen as Christlike, but *Ahimsa* has roots in India going back thousands of years.

In the Indian tradition several things are understood about nonviolence, and all of them apply to Jesus's version of turning the other cheek. First, the aim of nonviolence is ultimately to bring peace to yourself, to quell your own violence; the enemy outside serves only to mirror the enemy within. Second, your ability to be nonviolent depends on a shift in consciousness. Last, if you are successful in changing yourself, reality will mirror the change back to you.

Without these conditions, *Ahimsa* isn't spiritual or even effective. If someone full of desire for retaliation turns the other cheek to someone equally enraged, the only thing that will occur is more violence. Playing the part of a saint won't make a difference. But if a person in God-consciousness turns the other cheek, his enemy will be disarmed. I believe that in the bookstore I experienced a passing moment where that deep truth applied to me. *Ahimsa* is only one quality that belongs to God-consciousness. In Jesus's case, his mind contained them all.

The World Reborn

Jesus didn't want to keep the mystery of God-consciousness to himself. He constantly held out his vision to others, and he had a sense of urgency that was unmistakable. Life was going to be completely overturned, not in the distant future but very soon. The four gospels pick up this thread over and over. Jesus calls himself the New Adam, and his most articulate early follower, Saint Paul, declares that reality has changed completely because of Jesus's existence: "When anyone is united to Christ there is a new creature: his old life is over; a new life is already begun." (2 Corinthians 5:17)

Sometimes this verse is translated so that the phrase *a new creature* reads as *a new creation* or *a new world*. No other faith makes such sweeping, audacious claims. Early Christians took them literally, and belief in Jesus spread with astonishing speed throughout Jerusalem and beyond. To understand just how radical Jesus's vision actually was, we must consider its entirety. But in outline he intended to renew human existence in the following eight ways.

The New World of Jesus

1. *Nature*—The fallen state of nature would be restored to perfection. Paradise would return to earth; Eden would open its gates once more.
2. *Society*—War and strife would disappear. Human beings would live in a community based on God's grace, without the need for laws and punishment.
3. *Relationships*—People would relate as one soul to another, regardless of wealth and social position.
4. *Psychology*—Individuals would be motivated chiefly by love of God and a sense of worth based on God's love for his children.

5. *Emotions*—In place of anger, fear, and doubt, people would sense directly that they were loved, safe, and blessed.
6. *Behavior*—Living in a state of grace, people would no longer mistreat one another. Behavior would become peaceable and loving, not just within the immediate family, but toward neighbors and even strangers.
7. *Biology*—The human body itself would be transformed, no longer beset with illness.
8. *Metaphysics*—God would no longer be aloof from human affairs. He would become present on earth.

No more radical blueprint has ever been offered, and the first miracle in Jesus's story is that anyone believed him. If you select any item from the list, a staggering challenge lies ahead. Consider relationships. Jesus asked his followers to see themselves as souls rather than fallible individuals whose desires conflicted with one another. The equality of souls banishes the differences between rich and poor, men and women, the weak and the powerful. As a guide to everyday relationships, total equality was completely unworkable to begin with (no work bosses? no rulers? no church hierarchy?), but Jesus went much further. Souls receive everything directly from God. As Jesus declared in the Sermon on the Mount, a person living naturally, like the birds of the air or the lilies of the field, has no need to toil. God loves his children at least as much as he loves birds and flowers. He will give them an existence no less beautiful and carefree. Likewise, there is no need for souls to plan for the future, to store up wealth, or to be concerned with such vanities as fancy clothing. All these things would be provided for through Providence.

The implications for relationships were unfathomable. Could a farmer or fisherman go home to his wife and proclaim that he was never going to work again because God didn't want him to? Should households spend all their savings, trusting that God promised no more rainy days? How could they be sure that God would provide the necessities for their families? No wonder the pragmatists who took control over Christianity began to move away from the world as Jesus envisioned it.

Every aspect of existence would be equally affected by the new dispensation. The reality that Jesus had come to abolish was in every respect the opposite of what he envisioned.

Nature was widely experienced as the setting for endless toil and suffering. The average person eked out a meager existence, seeing no evidence of God's bounty and a great deal of evidence of his displeasure.

Society enforced its codes through rigid rules and harsh punishment. Human nature was so distrusted that in Leviticus, the book of the Old Testament concerned with living a righteous life, more than six hundred laws, rules, rituals, and religious obligations were set down.

Relationships were based on religious obligations also, trying to please an angry God rather than to find pleasure in one another. Women were subjugated, because they had brought the stain of sexuality and sin into the world.

Psychology was split into two contradictory parts. On the one hand, people were told to rejoice in God and to consider themselves chosen by him. On the other, the blemish of sin was ever present and affected each person from the moment of birth. Sin was more than an act against God; it was the primary condition of being human.

Emotions were considered unreliable and were distrusted. God himself was both loving and wrathful, and he could turn in an instant from one to the other. His children were just as unpredictable, and therefore the threat of punishment hovered constantly; if you wavered from complete faith in God, Satan would undermine you with temptation.

Behavior was essentially self-centered. Ideals existed, and people did their nominal best to be virtuous, but even then virtue applied only to "us" (family, tribe, religion) and not to "them" (a different family, tribe, religion). The way you acted toward your loved ones bore no relationship to the way you treated strangers, much less enemies.

Biology was outside human control. Sickness held sway over everyone and must therefore be a punishment from God. The indignities of aging and the terrifying prospect of death were also signs of God's displeasure.

Metaphysics was beyond the ken of ordinary people. Reading God's will and looking into his mind could be done only by priests, who were born into their station. They revealed the nature of the divine, and over time what they said became law.

It's easy to see why the new world Christ envisioned was so quickly abandoned after he died. It had to be modified by realists. No one could carry out the divine plan as articulated by Jesus, because everyone else was too deeply enmeshed in the old world. Its entanglements seemed inescapable. This enormous gap between real and ideal never closed. In the early nineteenth century, the great Danish philosopher Søren Kierkegaard tormented himself over the question of how to live as Jesus wished. Kierkegaard concluded, after years of suffering, that being a Christian was incompatible with ordinary middle-class life.

Kierkegaard entitled one of his most influential books *Either/Or* to illustrate how deep the schism was between a life of comfortable materialism and the radical values of Jesus. Yet Jesus himself was the very model of his teachings. Buddha said, "Whoever sees me sees the teaching," and the same is true of Jesus. He lived in Christ-consciousness, and his teaching grew directly out of his own state of awareness.

Jesus was capable of showing us the way to enlightenment. "Therefore you are to be perfect, as your heavenly Father is perfect."

(Matthew 5:43–48) Western culture took Jesus as its model, and his words gave Western culture values to live (and love) by. But we aren't living in an age of perfection—far from it—and the original impetus that Jesus gave us has become exhausted.

I heard a poignant story from a friend who long ago lapsed from the Anglican Church. When he recently returned to London, his trip coincided with Easter.

"Maybe it was nostalgia, but I was pulled to attend services at St. Paul's Cathedral," he told me. "I picked what is known as a singing service because the music is inspiring and the pomp has a moving kind of splendor, all crushed velvet robes and gold brocade for miles."

"Did the display fulfill your expectations?" I asked.

"No, but for a strange reason," he said. "The cathedral was full of tourists, the sermon was amplified over a loud microphone, and the presiding bishop droned on as if he couldn't be more bored.

"Right beside me a man in shabby clothes knelt on the cold marble floor for the entire hour. He prayed with his hands clasped, and he knew every line of the responses and prayers. I remembered that I used to be that way. It was one of the most profound things in my life to kneel in a great cathedral flooded with light."

"What stopped you from doing what that man was doing?" I asked.

"That's the thing. I was so tempted to fall on my knees, but he was the only one doing it, and several tourists were quietly taking his picture with their cell phones. I lost my nerve."

I think many Christians feel just as self-conscious when faced with the ritual and pomp of Easter and the overwhelming commercialism that surrounds Christmas. How are you supposed to participate—as one of the crowd enjoying the spectacle or as a lonely penitent before Christ? I don't presume to answer those questions for anyone; they are too personal, too wrapped up in each person's life history. And nothing in this book deprives you of participating in ritual and sacrament as you choose. My hope is to give you a glimpse of what I believe Jesus truly intended.

Enlightenment and consciousness-raising are considered Eastern concepts, not Christian ones. In India, countless gurus and spiritual masters have offered to teach ordinary people how to arrive at enlightenment, but it is only provincialism that divides spirituality East and West. Indians are scornful of outsiders coming in to skim the cream off ancient Vedic teachings, turning yoga into a weekend exercise class. Westerners are scornful of outsiders coming in to claim Jesus as a teacher on the order of Buddha and Muhammad instead of seeing him as the one and only Son of God.

Once we move outside the boundaries of dogmatic Catholicism and Hinduism, both positions can be seen to have deep flaws. Consciousness is universal, and if there is such a thing as God-consciousness, no one can be excluded from it. By the same token, no one can lay exclusive claim, either. If Jesus rose to the highest level of enlightenment, why should he be unique in that regard? Buddha may be his equal (hundreds of millions of followers believe so), along with Vedic rishis like Vasishtha and Vyassa, who didn't happen to have religions named after them.

Clearly Jesus did not have a provincial view of himself. Although a Jew and a rabbi (or teacher), he saw himself in universal terms. Indeed, he looked upon his arrival as the most important event in world history, an event whose significance could be judged only in God's time, not human time. For the ordinary person, time begins with birth and ends with death; epochs longer than a few generations dissolve into the mists of the past. Jesus thought timelessly. And two millennia later, he remains our contemporary, just as he intended.

"I Am the Light"

Is Jesus really all about enlightenment? The best way to find out is to examine his own words. In the gospels Jesus spent a great deal of time explaining himself to people who were mystified by him. He told them he was the Son of God, the Messiah, the Christ. But these have become Church words. They give Jesus a title, and yet what we want is something more personal.

Calling himself the Son of Man was personal—it denoted humility and a fate in common with everyday people. But Jesus tells us much more about himself when he says, "I am the Light." (John 9:5) Physically, light is what you see when you wake up in the morning. Mystically, it's what you see when you wake up to your soul. Light gives life, and it shows the way through the darkness. Jesus had all those things in mind. More thrilling, however, is his intention to raise others up to the same status, as when he said to his followers, "You are the Light of the world." (Matthew 5:12) Making others enlightened was his purpose, but a huge gulf yawned between Jesus and other people—the gulf between darkness and light—so his whole life amounts to one long struggle to make people see that they were in darkness and had to wake up.

We get a sense of the difficulty of the struggle in a famous confrontation between Jesus and a group of priests who set out to interrogate him. The incident starts out inspirationally:

> Once again Jesus addressed the people: "I am the Light of the world. No follower of mine shall wander in the dark; he shall have the light of life."
>
> *(John 8:12)*

Jesus had entered Jerusalem for the last time. Within hours he would be arrested by the Romans, on trial for his life. For the moment, however, his accusers are priests, who question him like lawyers.

> The Pharisees said to him, "You are witness in your own cause. Your testimony is not valid." Jesus replied, "My testimony is valid, even though I do bear witness about myself; because I know where I come from and where I am going. You do not know either where I come from or where I am going. You judge by worldly standards."

Here, with his teaching at its most mature, Jesus knows how enigmatic he seems to ordinary people, even the learned. For he goes on to say that the learned are the least able to understand either him or God:

> "I am the one who bears witness about myself, and the Father who sent me bears witness about me." They said to him therefore, "Where is your Father?" Jesus answered, "You know nei-

ther me nor my Father. If you knew me, you would know my
Father also."

This audacious claim that Jesus was the same as God infuriated
the priests. They couldn't comprehend that "I am God" is the simplest statement in the world for someone in God-consciousness.
(Simple as saying "I am awake" for someone who isn't asleep.) The
gospel writer senses that Jesus's meaning is mystical. Why else would
he say that he knows where he came from and where he is going? He
came from the light, and he is going back to it very soon. The gap
between Jesus and his listeners wasn't an empty space they could
jump across. Instead, the way he lived contradicted everything they
lived by, assaulting their beliefs and values. Jesus railed against the
law, money, and the ways of the world.

Instead of thinking that wisdom is unique to the Messiah, we
should take Jesus literally when he says, "You are the light of the
world." Jesus is describing our destiny as equal to his own. God-
consciousness is offering to open a path for us. Suffering isn't a matter
of breaking the law, renouncing money, or leaving the world. It's a
matter of seeing those obstacles as pure illusion. Let's look at the ingre-
dients that Jesus taught to be the essentials of a spiritual life.

1. *Meditation*—Going within to contact the silent mind.
2. *Contemplation*—Reflecting on the truth.
3. *Revelation*—Receiving spiritual insight.
4. *Prayer*—Asking for higher guidance.
5. *Grace*—Taking God into one's heart.
6. *Love*—Participating in divine love.
7. *Faith*—Believing in a higher reality.
8. *Salvation*—Realizing that you have a place in higher reality.
9. *Unity*—Becoming one with God.

Each of these can be interpreted through Jesus's constant reference to the light.

Meditation—The light exists inside everyone. When we go inside to find out who we are, we encounter the light and God at the same time.

Contemplation—Think about any object outside yourself or any event inside yourself. If you reflect upon it deeply enough, you will discover that everything is made of light. The inner and outer world are both reflections. Everything solid is a shadow; only the light is real.

Revelation—The light reveals itself when you see with the eyes of the soul. God is both hidden and revealed. The hidden God is darkness, the revealed God is light.

Prayer—Prayer is about finding the truth. If you ask God to show you the light, which is the essence of truth, he will. In the end, a prayer is simply the way the light asks to see itself.

Grace—The light can also be described as pure love. When acting as pure love, it bestows everything freely; this is grace.

Love—When your inner light is connected to God, love flows. Love is nothing but this living connection, in all its creativity and joy.

Faith—When you stop believing in the illusion of the material world and see everything for what it really is—light—you have faith. The reason all things are given to someone with faith is very simple: The light can shape itself into anything at will. Physical obstacles can't stop the free flow of light.

Salvation—You are redeemed when you move into the light. You've escaped your false self and arrived at your true self. The false or unredeemed self was trapped in physical limitation. The true self is as unbounded as the light.

Unity—Physical boundaries make it impossible to be united with God, but there are no boundaries in the light. Therefore, once you realize you are the light, nothing stands between you and God.

None of these statements is a metaphor for something transcendent and out of reach. Who hasn't lain in the grass on a summer night and sensed something thrilling just beyond the sky? Or gazed into a lover's eyes and found a quivering thrill behind their warmth? Glimpses of beauty and love are glimpses of the light. You can align yourself with God-consciousness at any given moment by pursuing these glimpses. The results might be strange, however. Whereas I turn on the television and see carnage in the Middle East with road-side bombs and blood everywhere, Jesus would see only light, and his compassion would go out to the suffering, not because of their pain so much as for their inability to be in the light with him, since there they would find the end of suffering. Perception creates reality, and all of Jesus's sayings have one thing in common: They try to make our perceptions shift.

The trick, in fact, is to take Jesus literally. After centuries of theology, our minds find it difficult to consider him without the trappings of a messiah. When he says, "I am the Way, and the Truth, and the Light," the capital letters aren't just a holdover from an archaic form of English; they are Jesus's patent on God. Yet the light is your own consciousness, here and now, in the messy present tense. If you think about going to a movie this afternoon, that thought came from the light. The same is true if you are thinking about your next meal, or sex, or how to stop smoking. What makes Jesus so difficult for us to grasp is that he never veers away from the purity of the light. He has no choice. God-consciousness creates its own reality. I often think that we are incredibly fortunate to have as much understanding of Jesus as we do. He could just as easily have been dismissed as insane.

Try, for example, to understand his famous saying "Resist not evil." Over the years, this teaching has become diluted. It has been watered down into a kind of compassionate passivity, a way to walk away from bullies instead of fighting back. By turning the other cheek, we feel morally superior because we haven't added to the violence in the world, even when provoked. But the relevant passage from the New Testament is even more radical. I have reworded it in modern words:

> "You've been taught an eye for an eye and a tooth for a tooth, but I say don't resist evil. If someone hits you, let him hit you twice. If someone sues you in court to get your coat, give it to him and your cloak, too. If someone forces you to go one mile, go two. If someone asks you for something, give it to him. If he wants to borrow money, don't turn your back."
>
> *(Matthew 5:38–42)*

These dictates seem completely unworkable. An eye for an eye, the teaching that Jesus wanted to overturn, remains much easier to follow. The moment someone is branded as evil (terrorists, Nazis, mass murderers, pedophiles, and so forth), the natural reaction seems to be revenge; we assume that despite Jesus's urgings, we have every right to exact punishment. The current War on Terror is based on this notion. Yet any form of fighting against contradicts Jesus, a fact that right-wing Christian hawks conveniently ignore.

"Resist not evil," if carried out in real life, would lead to a society of forgiveness. Horrendous notion! If we went around forgiving everybody, either the evil people would completely take over, dominating us, or they might forgive us in return and stop being evil. This second option, which Jesus perhaps had in mind, is unthinkable, if not crazy. To demonstrate that "Resist not evil" isn't insane, Jesus lived out his own teaching. He submitted to an unjust trial, persecution, and finally violent death. Christians worship him for doing so, since it led to the resurrection. Surrender proved to be Jesus's ultimate weapon. But the fact that Jesus is worshipped for not resisting evil hasn't carried the day for us ordinary mortals—we continue to live, by and large, by the very law he preached against: an eye for an eye.

The missing element, as always, is consciousness. You cannot live by "Resist not evil" without being in a higher state of consciousness. Fortunately, to the extent that you rise toward God-consciousness, evil withdraws, leaving you invulnerable.

Evil is everything when you are susceptible to it; it is nothing when you aren't. These are the two poles of spiritual existence, the beginning and the end of the journey. In between are many steps, but Jesus doesn't fill them in. Perhaps in real life he did, because the scant words he left to us, those his followers could remember and write down, amount to less than two or three hours if read one after the other. However, the wisdom traditions of the world can fill in the blanks for us. In Buddhism, in the ancient Vedic writings of India, and in the lives of Christian saints, we find abundant evidence that awareness can grow in the direction of God-consciousness, and we see how it can do so.

How to "Resist Not Evil"

Meditation—Sit every day and find the silence inside yourself. In this silence, there is peace without anger. There is no evil, no attachment to revenge or righteous indignation. With practice, you learn to identify yourself with this place. It becomes natural to master anger, an energy like any other. When this happens, evil begins to release you from its hold.

Contemplation—The mind plays a large part in how you react to evil. The more excited your mind, the more threatening evil becomes. The more victimized you feel, the more aggressive evil becomes. The more you fear evil and see it everywhere, the more you will have to defend yourself. But these perceptions can shift. In the larger scheme, good and evil are constantly at war; neither ultimately gains the upper hand. Therefore, you can't end evil, you can only decide if you want to fight in the war or not. But if you decide not to fight, your mind will lose interest in evil, and as it does, evil will retreat.

Revelation—When you fear evil, you are certain that it must be real. This certainty forces you to engage in the eternal struggle between good and evil. No amount of passive resistance will extricate you, except perhaps temporarily. But if you can see that the war between good and evil is nothing but a play of light and shadow, your certainty about the existence of evil will fade away. To see through the mask of evil, search for the light that is the essence of everything. The fruit of this search is revelation; the light reveals itself of its own accord.

Prayer—Ask to see what lies behind evil. This doesn't have to be a philosophical request. What you want is a glimpse behind the disguises we all wear when we feel angry, victimized, hostile, and aggressive. These emotions are insubstantial, convincing for only a moment. Yet we are so intimidated by other people's emotions and so convinced by our own that we lose sight of the underlying reality. By praying to whatever deity or higher self you believe in, you are essentially making a connection with reality, asking to be reminded that illusion isn't real.

Grace—Grace replaces evil with love. You cannot do this when you feel afraid, angry, or victimized. However, as you are working through your negativity, keep in mind that what lies on the other side is a gift. Evil doesn't leave a void behind when it goes, it leaves a space to be filled by God.

Love—Every enemy is a symbol of your own loveless state. The absence of love gets filled by evil, in the form of conflict and warring emotions. By returning to a state of love, you rob evil of a place to live. In practical terms this means pushing away the habit of judgment. Whenever you are tempted to call someone evil, accept the negative energy as your own and then move it out of your mind and body. This requires patience; it doesn't happen all at once. However, if you undertake this work, its results are lasting. Love is more powerful than evil because it alone is real.

Faith—Faith is required when you are in a state of suffering. Nothing is more convincing than pain, and when it is present, words can't make it go away. Pain is too physical and too present. But despite its intensity, pain is only temporary. Evil depends on our forgetting this fact. If it couldn't inflict pain, evil would have no power at all. Therefore, when caught in the throes of any pain, keep faith. Realize that there is a reality beyond our present misery. You are that reality, and you will return to it as your suffering lessens.

Salvation—When you can step outside of your own suffering, you are saved. In spiritual terms, salvation is the same as being rescued physically. Physical danger puts us in a state of chaos, hurt, fear of danger, and panic. All these conditions are reflected in your mind: You resort to images of disaster whenever mental threats appear. Therefore, to be saved from suffering, you must find a place that is neither physical nor mental. Jesus calls this place the Kingdom of God, or the soul. The label is less important than finding experience. Step by step, each person must locate an inner state that is free from images of pain; in that state lies redemption.

Unity—All the previous steps serve one purpose, to blur the line between good and evil. In the beginning, these are stark opposites. We experience good through pleasure, peace, well-being, safety. We experience evil through pain, struggle, restriction, and fear. We naturally seek the one and run away from the other. What we don't see is that these "natural" tendencies belong to a state of awareness that has been conditioned over time. In other words, they are self-created. By gaining knowledge of the self, you also learn how to create new things in place of the old. As regards evil, the new thing you must create is the absence of duality. No more dark versus light. No more fixed boundaries to divide safe from unsafe, God from Satan, self from nonself. As these boundaries fade, nothing remains but one reality, a boundless state known as God. To the extent that you can dissolve your own fearful limitations, you get closer to God-consciousness, and in the same process you rob evil of its seeming reality.

This is only the briefest outline of how a person can move beyond evil, but I believe it is what Jesus meant when he said, "Resist not evil." Behind the appearance of craziness lies profound wisdom, yet we get only a hint of that in the few words recorded by the gospels. The full teaching needs to be unpacked from the suitcase, as it were, and laid out in detail.

The Gnostic Gospels

I met a journalist from India recently who screwed up his face when I told him that I was writing about Jesus. I asked him why. "I loved being a Christian when I was a child back home," he said. "But being a Christian in America makes me queasy." It turns out that his faith was the product of missionaries, whose presence in India dates back to Saint Thomas—the same doubting Thomas who was invited by the resurrected Christ to touch his wounds—who reportedly sailed to the southern tip of India in 52 AD and founded the first church there. In one of the ancient churches in the state of Kerala, parishioners still adhere to Aramaic and Syrian rituals.

When innocence is lost, mystery vanishes with it. Skeptics aren't alone in wondering if the miracles that Jesus performed—

raising the dead, turning water into wine, or walking on the Sea of Galilee—aren't exaggerations of real-life events. Conversion can be a tough sell, and it helps if the story you are selling contains magic.

We aren't the first people to rebel against established religion, nor is this the first time church worship has fallen away in the face of doubt. Among early Christian sects, some challenged the notion that praying to Christ was enough to reach God. They chafed at church authority, believing it was up to each Christian to find God through personal knowledge of him and thus to attain enlightenment. They felt that enlightenment, not salvation in Heaven, was Jesus's mission. Here is how one of their most lucid scriptures, known as the Gospel of Truth, puts it:

> Forgetfulness did not exist with the Father, although it existed because of him. What exists in him is knowledge, which was revealed so that forgetfulness might be destroyed and that they might know the Father. Since forgetfulness existed because they did not know the Father, if they then come to know the Father, from that moment on forgetfulness will cease to exist.

Forgetfulness, not sin, is seen as the root cause of error, our loss of contact with God. We return to God by remembering him, and as memory returns, each of us is restored to knowledge of the Divine. Because knowledge was so crucial to these early sects, they became known as Gnostics, from the Greek word *gnosis,* or "knowledge."

You can immediately see the appeal of Gnosticism to the modern mind. It sounds liberal, nonauthoritarian, and open-ended. The Gospel of Truth accuses conventional Christians of missing the whole point of Jesus, falling into blind worship instead of trying to seek enlightenment:

Through [Jesus, God] enlightened those who were in darkness
because of forgetfulness. He enlightened them and gave them
a path. And that path is the truth which he taught them.

To our ears, this sounds like a doctrine of personal growth, and
that makes the Gospel of Truth extremely appealing. The Jesus it
portrays has knowledge of the All, an imperishable fullness that is
the divine gift to humanity, if only people will open their eyes.

[Jesus] became a guide, quiet and in leisure. In the middle of a
school he came and spoke the Word, as a teacher. Those who
were wise in their own estimation came to put him to the test.
But he discredited them as empty-headed people. They hated
him because they really were not wise men.

Here we glimpse the universal theme of Gnosticism: a war
between Sophia ("wisdom") and the forces of darkness that has been
waged since the dawn of creation and exists inside each of us. This
inner conflict has left us blind to truth, but we can rediscover it
because in his fullness (*Pleroma*), the Father provides a path back to
the All, which can never be lost. Change a few terms here, and we
could be reading the Vedas as recounted by the ancient Indian seers.

I've been surprised at the discomfiture from all quarters when I
began writing about Jesus. No one wants to be shaken in his belief,
or lack of it. One nervous friend said, "So you must be a Gnostic?
That's the only line you could really take, right?"

No, I explained, I wasn't a Gnostic. But I understood the
comment. Ever since the discovery of a huge cache of early scriptural documents in Egypt in 1945, renegades and reformers in
the Church have found ammunition for their causes. The Gnostic
Gospels, as they are known, include the Gospel of Truth, the Gospel

of Thomas (a book that came closest, perhaps, to being included in the canon of the New Testament), the Gospel of Philip, and other scriptures found at other times and places, such as the now famous—or infamous—Gospel of Mary Magdalene, discovered in 1896 but not published until 1955.

These scriptures represent an alternate road, which Christianity never took. Suppressed and eventually wiped out by the ascendant Catholic Church, the Gnostics rejected authority, preferring to walk an individual path guided by revelation. If my goal is a higher state of consciousness, why isn't this book Gnostic?

There was no Christian sect known as the Gnostics, at least not the way we can identify Protestants or the Greek Orthodox. The term was invented by modern scholars. It now has a positive connotation, but historically, the Gnostics were despised as heretics. In fact, before the discovery of the Gnostic Gospels, almost all that was known about Gnostics came from Church fathers who reviled Gnostics and worked toward their extermination. Second, the Gnostic Gospels expound no uniform belief. The documents known as the Nag Hammadi library, after the town in Upper Egypt where they were discovered in a cave, consist of thirteen codices dating from 390 AD. Many are heavily damaged, in addition to being written in a kind of secret code full of symbols and arcane references.

Historically, 390 AD is early for a surviving scripture, which allows the Nag Hammadi scrolls to lay claim to as much authenticity as various versions of the four gospels; the scrolls are an esoteric jumble. We do gain from them certain intriguing facts: The early church was deeply divided; it didn't necessarily have a hierarchy of priests, but when it did, women were allowed to participate as priests. Each person in the congregation could stand up and preach when moved by the spirit. Individual experience dominated over written doctrine.

Renegades and reformers welcomed the Gnostic Gospels, because they contended that Christianity would benefit from allowing women into the clergy, among other controversial issues. Moving away from central authority also suits the modern temperament: If higher knowledge of God can be gained by each of us, why should we allow the Church to quash our efforts? It's hard to resist the enlightened body of believers glowingly depicted in the Gospel of Truth:

> They came to know and they were known. They were glorified and they gave glory. In their heart, the living book of the Living was manifest, the book which was written in the thought and in the mind of the Father. . . .

Yet the freedom offered by Gnosticism presented its own perils. A Pentecostal church in the rural South where the congregation speaks in tongues and the preacher espouses his own eccentric brand of Christianity is pure Gnosticism. Such congregations have taken up handling rattlesnakes to prove that their faith places them beyond harm. Others believe in child sexuality or revile the "mixing of the races." And even if we set aside the more bizarre possibilities that might arise from Gnosticism, the Gnostic Gospels themselves are a disorganized mix at best, including Jesus along with such religious figures as Seth, Sophia, various demiurges (creators below the level of God), and strange cults that have no value today, except to obscure an already obscure theology.

We may find allure in the freedom of nonrational thought, for that is where art, faith, intuition, and love are born. But each bright thing has its shadow side, and pure Gnosticism doesn't offer safeguards from the darkness. The early Church fathers have been demonized for exterminating the Gnostic sects, as well they should be. But they were wrestling with their own darkness at the same time;

the Gnostics were only a symbol for the inner demons that created so much suffering, which was all the more painful because the Church fathers were promising that Jesus had rid the world of sin once and for all. No one can look around the world, then or now, and believe such a claim. But we can find a body of teachings that Jesus left behind that isn't clouded by other people's desperate wish for a messiah. In the gospels themselves lie the materials for an inner journey that will be richer than anything offered by the Gnostics.

"The Kingdom of God Is Within"

No matter what version of Jesus you accept, the goal of a Christian life is to reach the Kingdom of God. Millions of believers hold that this means going to Heaven after you die. But Jesus is much more ambiguous than that. There is just as much evidence in the gospels that reaching the Kingdom of God means arriving at a higher level of consciousness. As is so often the case, you can read scripture many ways. But I think the argument for higher consciousness is by far the most persuasive.

Let's ask the most basic question first. Where is the Kingdom of God located? Jesus's listeners were Jewish, and traditionally an afterlife wasn't part of their religion, much less a Heaven where rewards are meted out to the righteous. We are so used to the concept of Heaven, whether as believers or as skeptics, that it's hard to imagine a time when the concept was new and controversial. Jesus painted Heaven as a source of rest for the weary and balm for the suffering, which was well received by his listeners, who lived lives of physical hardship and unending hard labor. The Book of Genesis told Jews that this wasn't God's original intention for humanity;

toiling in the dust was the punishment bestowed on Adam and Eve after they were driven from the Garden of Eden.

Jesus thus closes the circle, bringing back Eden through the forgiveness of sin. Since the original garden was full of every delight, Heaven must be the same. Christian tradition paints the Kingdom of God as paradise, a banquet hall for the starving presided over by a smiling Father. In mundane terms, it's the warm home that the master welcomes his workers into after a hard day tending the vineyard. Modern life may be more comfortable, but still we yearn for this place of refuge and rest. Also, Christianity has always focused on the weak and poor, whose longing for rest and relief certainly hasn't changed since Jesus's time.

What does the Bible have to say about the God of popular imagination, presiding over his kingdom from a throne above the clouds? The word *throne* is found 166 times in the Old Testament, only 7 times in the four gospels, and 37 times in the Book of Revelation. Thus Jesus was not the source of our kinglike image of God. In his few references to God's throne, Jesus echoes the Old Testament. This is common practice by the writers of the gospels, who were intent on making sure that their candidate for Messiah fulfilled all the requirements of the prophets and supported the tenet that the Jews were God's chosen ones. At one point, he says:

> Truly I tell you, at the renewal of all things, when the Son of Man
> is seated on the throne of his glory, you who have followed me
> will also sit on twelve thrones, judging the twelve tribes of Israel.
>
> *(Matthew 19:28)*

This repeats a promise found over and over in the Old Testament:

> . . . they now stand before the divine throne and live the life of
> eternal blessedness.
>
> *(4 Maccabees 17:18)*

But the Lord sits enthroned forever, he has established his throne for judgment.

(Psalms 9:7)

I dwelt in the highest heavens, and my throne was in a pillar of cloud.

(Ecclesiasticus 24:4)

The last passage isn't God speaking, however, but the virtue of Wisdom praising herself poetically. Without a doubt, however, the Old Testament writers wanted to put the coming Messiah and the kings of Israel on the same throne, one that came directly from God.

So why do millions of Christians believe in a literal Heaven and a literal throne of God? The New Testament reverts to the literal usage at the very end, long after Jesus's death, in the Book of Revelation, with its nearly forty references to "the throne." Revelation is highly pictorial, unfolding the Day of Judgment (that is, the end of the world) with riveting and terrifying imagery.

We do not know who wrote this book of the Bible; it is traditionally credited to the same John who wrote the Gospel of John, supposedly when he was exiled for his beliefs to the Greek island of Patmos. But no real proof of that exists. Certainly the Kingdom of God described in Revelation has little or no authority from Jesus himself, although he does refer to final judgment and the division of the evil and the righteous. I think believers cling to Revelation because it fills a void. Jesus didn't dramatize the End of Days. He offered nothing as visually gripping as the book with seven seals, the Four Horsemen of the Apocalypse, the opening of graves and souls rising out of the ground. Jesus's promise to return to earth wasn't nearly that cinematic. Since on the whole he refused to dramatize Judgment Day, just as he refused to make Heaven a literal place, shouldn't we respect that?

When Jesus isn't mouthing the words expected of him by the writers of the gospels, he argues against worldliness as being unfit for God. He severely rebukes the priests in the temple who require offerings of spices and gold:

> "You blind fools! For which is greater, the gold, or the sanctuary that has made the gold sacred? . . . Whoever swears by the sanctuary, swears by it and by the one who dwells in it; and whoever swears by heaven, swears by the throne of God and by the one who is seated upon it."
>
> *(Matthew 25: 17–22)*

Here Jesus is pointing out that God dwells invisibly in the holy objects of the temple and that his presence constitutes holiness, not the objects themselves. The same holds true of Heaven. The physical place we imagine is a husk; the real Kingdom of God cannot be seen. All of this supports Jesus's explicit declaration, "The Kingdom of God is within you." The statement is even more emphatic in context:

> And when he was demanded of the Pharisees, when the kingdom of God should come, he answered them and said, "The kingdom of God cometh not with observation. Neither shall they say, Lo here! or, Lo there! for, behold, the kingdom of God is within you."
>
> *(Luke 17:20–21)*

These words can be seen as the impetus for the entire Gnostic movement, with its scorn for outer trappings and its insistence that all contact with God or Christ must be individual. Only inner transformation could bring about Christ's vision of the Kingdom of God on earth, which was the Messiah's ultimate mission. If the Gnostics were correct, the Book of Revelation would be wrong.

Jesus will not return physically to raise the dead from their graves. Instead, the Second Coming will be a shift in consciousness that renews human nature by raising it to the level of the divine.

Centuries after the Gnostics were eradicated by the official church, the Kingdom of God kept its blurry boundaries. To some it became a wish fulfillment, a utopia based on love, tolerance, and understanding that would sweep away and replace the corrupt material world. In his 1894 manifesto, *The Kingdom of God Is Within You,* Tolstoy proposed creating such utopian communities without waiting for the Second Coming.

Tolstoy took Christ personally, seeking him through a simple, literal adherence to his teachings. Theology was to be swept away, and the believer was to take on faith that life could be organized by loving your neighbor, turning the other cheek, not resisting evil, and so forth. Particularly in America there has been a strong tradition of utopian Christian communities, and some still persist, but any attempt to impose an ideal society upon the framework of lower consciousness is bound to fail.

Medieval monastic life was based on much the same ideal, but even when sealed off from the world, such communities succeed only through the great sacrifice of everyday desires and aspirations.

Utopian communities and monasteries take Jesus far away from everyday existence. I don't think that he had an isolated spiritual elite in mind. When Jesus said that the Kingdom of God is within, he meant within everyone. This would be in keeping with his injunction to love your enemies. The same God is in them as in you. Killing an enemy would be the same as killing an aspect of God as well as of yourself.

So, did Jesus mean that the Kingdom of God is in us at every moment or only after we seek it out? Why is God silent and seemingly absent for millions of people? The deeper you go into the matter, the harder it becomes to find a livable way to follow Jesus's words. One can't reduce his teaching to a simple matter of looking inward instead of outward. Jesus didn't close the door to any version of the Kingdom mentioned in the Bible.

God as Image and Idea

There's an intriguing approach to this problem that isn't scriptural at all but scientific. We get tantalizing clues from medical research that all pictorial images of God and Heaven are actual mental constructs imprinted on our brains by society. Thousands of people have had near death experiences and returned with descriptions of God and Heaven. For the literalists to be right, these descriptions would need to agree with one another, but they don't. There are discernible patterns. Young children tend to report that Heaven is pastoral and contains baby animals at play. Adults most often report green pastures also, although a vast uncloudy blue sky is just as common. Very few come back with detailed descriptions matching the hierarchy of angels mounting to the throne that Dante popularized in his *Paradiso,* but that was a theological creation of the Middle Ages, taking off from Revelation, not Jesus himself.

The key point is that people see what they expect to see, and as cultures vary, so does the location of God. In the East, the complexly layered Bardo of Buddhists and the innumerable Lokas of Hindus replace the Christian Heaven. Since all of these visions are mental events, it's hard to escape the conclusion that they might also be mental creations.

The same holds true for our imagery of God. Jesus mocks the priests who think they know who God is. His audience included many other kinds of people with their own private conception of God. In general, a devout Jew would have adhered to the orthodoxy of the Bible, but the Old Testament doesn't depict God as a person in the first place. Moses raged against his brother Aaron for raising a golden calf to be worshipped, because idolatry defiled the basic principle in Judaism that God was abstract and unimaginable. He transcends physicality, to the point that his mystery cannot be thought of or spoken (the very name Yahweh had to be written in code or omitted entirely, for fear of blasphemy). Human nature being what it is, however, ordinary people continued to turn God into a benign father, an irascible punisher, an impartial judge—in other words, all manner of human being. God came to be created in man's image, not the other way around.

Jesus resorts to these images, using the word *father* quite frequently but resorting to other images as he needs to. Doesn't this affirm that he, like an everyday believer now, thought of God as a person? I would argue that "father" is actually a substitute for something ineffable. In the Hebrew tradition, the sacred name of God, Yahweh, could not be written or spoken. All references were by indirection (this tradition is still maintained among certain believers, both Jewish and Christian, who write "G-d" in place of "God"). Various synonyms entered common usage, such as King, Creator, Lord, Almighty, and Father. It was understood that these synonyms were stand-ins. Today, people say "God the Father" as if they are referring to a real entity. I don't think Jesus would agree. He is referring to something much more mystical when he says that he and the Father are one or that he is in the Father and the Father is in him.

It's disconcerting how often he returns to God as a source of punishment; one would think that the Old Testament judge, quick to anger and reluctant to forgive, hadn't budged. Jehovah didn't vacate the Bible just because a new testament arrived to replace the old. Christianity took advantage of the stubborn patriarchal punisher and his refusal to step down in favor of a loving God. The emphasis only shifted, to Christ as the redeemer of sin, the new Adam who would lead humankind back into grace even though they deserved punishment. Sin remained in the world, despite Jesus's absolute promise of forgiveness, and it was necessary to retain, as he did, the old scheme of Heaven and Hell.

Finally, the Kingdom of God could never be one thing. It had to serve too many purposes and was entangled in too many aspects of traditional religion. I think the only way to solve the riddles posed by the Kingdom of God is to say that God exists in different places depending on your level of consciousness. This becomes critical on the spiritual path, because as your own awareness shifts, God does, too.

The Path to Heaven

The most reliable thing we can say is that Jesus pointed the way to a seeker's Heaven. Finding God was a mystery, but in more mundane terms it was a process, not a leap or a promise that would be automatically fulfilled at the sound of the last trumpet. Perhaps this was a message delivered only to close disciples, for there are places in the gospels when Jesus does promise a reward to the righteous based simply on faith in him. In the Beatitudes, only humility is needed: "Blessed are the poor in spirit, for theirs is the kingdom of heaven." (Matthew 5:3) Christians still were left to figure out how to live according to Jesus's words, and the simplest injunctions proved harder than anything else. Over the centuries, three paths emerged.

The path of devotion is based on prayer, constant worship, and love of Christ. On this path, Christians draw near to God by fixing their minds on him. Jesus is the human face of God, and devotees fix their minds on him as the perfect model of the devout life.

The path of service is based on charity, altruism, and humility. The guiding principles are two: Love thy neighbor as thyself, and do unto others as you would have them do unto you. Christians aim at selflessness, offering up their worldly life in humble service to the poor. Jesus serves as the model of service by his constant attention to the poor and sick.

The path of contemplation is monastic, reclusive, and impoverished. The world is renounced completely, sometimes in favor of complete retreat into silence. One's life is given over to seeking the Kingdom of God within. Jesus serves as the model for this path by his inner communion with God.

One finds the same paths widely followed in other spiritual traditions, but nowhere are believers at such a disadvantage as Christians find themselves. In the gospels, Jesus speaks very few words regarding everyday life. No other faith has such meager explanations of what the founder meant for his followers to do. Moreover, Jesus speaks in absolutes, as we have abundantly seen, and his voice comes from an eternal place, only rarely from the everyday world.

All three paths are adaptable to the search for God-consciousness. The significant change is that your devotion, service, and contemplation of God are directed toward the higher self, or soul. Where traditional Christianity uses Christ as the means to reach God's presence, the path to God-consciousness uses awareness.

Specifically, we follow Jesus's words, repeated often in the gospels, about the need to wake up and to remain awake.

> "Therefore, keep awake—for you do not know when the master of the house will come, in the evening, or at midnight, or at cockcrow, or at dawn."
>
> *(Mark 13:35)*

When we join this injunction with the one about the Kingdom of God being within, the implication is that going within requires a person to wake up, also. In fact, that's the only way to live any spiritual path to the fullest. The traditional ways of devotion, service, and contemplation don't actually solve the problem of Jesus's contradiction between inner and outer life. Tolstoy was right: If you take Jesus at his word, your life must be realigned completely, away from worldly ways toward godly ones.

Because he is so absolute, Jesus doesn't offer a path of devotion that consists of daily prayer and piety to God. He wants total, unswerving devotion: You shall love the Lord your God with all your heart, and with all your soul, and with all your mind. In other words, every thought must be of God and every action directed toward him. Such a teaching is unworkable except for the most pious of recluses. The same holds true for the complete selflessness required on the path of service and the total fixation on spirituality required on the path of contemplation. But denying the world is a path to extinction, which no one can advocate. Nor can we assume that Jesus wanted us to annihilate our egos and personalities in the name of God. It's more reasonable to assume that reaching Heaven requires an unfolding process.

If you were able to meet Jesus today as he was in real life, there would be a gap between your level of awareness and his— we know that this is true when we encounter spiritually inspired people who are far less enlightened than Jesus, the saintly among us whose compassion reflects back our own spiritual shortcomings. If you were to follow Jesus after meeting him, you would have to try to close this gap, setting you on a path that unfolds over time. The same holds true without a flesh-and-blood Jesus; the same gap needs to be closed between your present state of awareness and God-consciousness. Devotion, service, and contemplation remain viable ways to transform yourself, yet even the most devout Christians fall into the trap of believing that they don't have to transform themselves inwardly, that performing enough acts of devotion (attending church, praying, giving to the poor, and the like) will suffice or that doing charitable work among the poor and sick, or thinking about God as often as possible, will be sufficient. Jesus warns us against this trap when he speaks, in parable form, about seed that falls on waste ground and doesn't sprout. The seed is his teaching; the waste ground is a mind unprepared to receive the truth.

What Jesus doesn't elaborate upon is how waste ground can be made fertile. He says only that some people receive a bit of the truth, some a great deal, and some none at all. Let's assume that you and I can absorb some of the truth, rather than all, or none. In this regard, we fit into the category of Jesus's disciples. We are neither hopeless nor fully realized in God. We turn to Jesus because he understands the territory of the unknown, the source not only of a messiah but of the soul itself.

Part Two

THE GOSPEL OF
ENLIGHTENMENT

READING WHAT JESUS SAID

When Jesus speaks most directly about enlightenment, he touches on many diverse topics, often briefly but with great power. I've selected ten subjects that cover every significant teaching about consciousness spoken in Jesus's own voice. The ten subject headings are as follows:

Love and Grace
Faith
Revelation and Redemption
Jesus and the Self
Meditation
Contemplation
Prayer
Karma—Reaping and Sowing
The World as Illusion
Unity

Most of these topics will seem familiar. Faith, love, and redemption remain important on the path to enlightenment, just as they are in traditional Christianity. But at least two topics—Karma and the world as illusion—will sound foreign to Christian ears. But Jesus raised the topic of Karma when he said, "As you sow, so shall you reap," and he touched on the world as illusion when he said, "Be in the world, but not of it." These are familiar sayings, into which Jesus delved more deeply than most people realize. He may not have used the Sanskrit word *Karma,* but there is abundant evidence that he had already incorporated the lessons of Karma into his own worldview.

The four gospels are arranged to tell a story; however, in so doing, they jumble together many topics. In their desire to make every utterance sound eternal, the gospel writers often ignored time and place. Jesus's words aren't even given in chronological order, which might have told us how his ideas developed. For example, did Jesus always bless the poor and condemn the rich, or did those teachings occur at specific times, addressing specific people? Because Jesus is made to speak for all time, he floats in a kind of intentional otherworldliness.

I had to pick and choose among hundreds of verses, so I've tried to reflect the whole range of what Jesus had to say, even when he sounds negative or discouraging. For contrary to the conventional picture we have of a smiling, benign Jesus, he was capable of anger, harshness, and even dismissal of those who couldn't or wouldn't understand him.

Translations of the Bible can be a thorny issue. I had over a dozen translations of the New Testament to choose from. The differences among them can be startling. Take one of Jesus's most stirring calls to the faithful: "From that time Jesus began to preach and say, 'Repent, for the kingdom of heaven is at hand.'" (Matthew 4:17) Those are the words of the King James Bible, at once terse and eloquent, speaking directly to the heart of sinners. Is the same meaning conveyed, or just hinted at, by an updated rendering in which Jesus told people, "Turn to God and change the way you think and act, for the kingdom of heaven is near!" (Good Word translation) Despite the exclamation point at the end, Jesus sounds timid; he isn't even preaching, but giving advice. Or should we turn to a literal translation, with all its awkwardness and lack of grace? "From that time began Jesus to proclaim and to say, 'Reform ye, for come nigh has the reign of the heaven.'" (Young Literal translation)

I settled on the New Revised Standard Version because it updates the incomparable language of the King James Bible without totally modernizing it. There is no need to sacrifice the perfect simplicity of a verse like "Blessed are the poor in spirit, for theirs is the kingdom of heaven" (Matthew 5:3), as long as the meaning is clear. When necessary, however, I've altered wordings slightly for the sake of making the meaning clearer.

As a side note, the four gospels weren't written in eloquent Greek, and Jesus himself spoke a dialect of Aramaic peculiar to the area he came from, the northern region of Galilee. Greek was the language of the marketplace in the eastern Roman Empire. Hawkers of fish and linen would shout out their wares in this rough lingua franca; hagglers would bargain in it; foreign traders from opposite sides of the Mediterranean would resort to it so that they could understand one another. This meant that the language had to be basic. As a result, the four gospels are direct and plain. They don't go in for niceties of expression. Many verses take the form of "Jesus said A, and then he said B. Jesus said C, and then he said D." This plain construction suits Jesus, who spoke starkly and dramatically in order to wake people up. Opening the New Testament at random, one finds that Mark 21 contains the word *and* fifteen times in the first ten verses, including the following: "The disciples went and did as Jesus had directed them; they brought the donkey and the colt, and put their cloaks on them, and he sat on them." (Matthew 21:6–7)

Jesus's vision was so breathtaking that it inspired a new religion, but without the lens of higher consciousness, these teachings seem to be mere fantasy, a distant hope that will be fulfilled, if ever, only in Heaven. Christians want to feel that their religion is unique, which is certainly achieved by claiming the one and only Son of God. But by the same token, they risk being left out of the great human project, which began centuries before Christ and continues to this day. This is the project of transcending the physical world to reach the realm of the soul.

Love and Grace

Jesus identified completely with love, and he is absolute about it: "By this sign everyone will know that you are my disciples, that you love one another." (John 13:35) *Love* is certainly the word most strongly associated with Jesus (even though he used it only about forty times in the four gospels). If they remember nothing else about Jesus, people carry around his saying, Love thy neighbor as thyself.

The earliest writings after the Crucifixion, such as the letters of Paul, are ecstatic with the promise of God's love and feverish to bring that message to the world. It was as if God had forgotten the human race until Jesus came to inject divine love back into everyday life. He himself puts it that way, calling love his "new commandment." Although Judaism already commanded people to love God (the Song of Solomon is as ecstatic about love as anything in the New Testament), Jesus treats love as something radical, a life-changing event. Love will bring God back into our existence. Love will make peace with our enemies and bring joy into our hearts.

What makes love new? This question needs to be posed in every generation; it's the seed of the spiritual quest. If you cannot discover what divine love actually is, no temple can supply it for you second-hand. Like every organized religion, Christianity long ago abandoned love as a radical path to transformation, paying ceremony and respect to Jesus's words about loving thy neighbor while sanctioning war and intolerance. In this way the Church succeeded in becoming acceptable to society, with its age-old habit of violence, but it never solved the riddle posed by Jesus's cardinal tenet: How could a person possibly love anyone else—neighbor, enemy, or family—as much as he loves himself?

At the level of the ego this challenge is impossible to solve. "I" will always be more important than "you." Even deep romantic love, which in the beginning seems to merge two people completely, can turn to division and hatred if my beloved betrays me. The intensity of a mother's love for her child can be self-serving or turn the child into a spoiled brat. The root of the problem is that divine love is divided from human love by a great gap. As we have already seen, this is a chasm of consciousness, and only consciousness can fill it.

Human love depends upon relationships. The people who are closest to me get my love; those who are far away from me don't. In my relationships, I expect to give and to receive. Others must deserve the love I hold out, and if they don't, I withdraw it. By contrast, divine love is freely given and unearned. God's grace transcends any relationship. God cannot relate any differently to one person than to another. Jesus makes this point very clearly when he says that God loves and forgives the wicked. They haven't earned love through any action or love directed toward God. All they had to do was to exist. To be is to be loved by God.

Yet there are times when Jesus demands that people obey the law of Moses and be punished for their sins. He says that they must believe in him as Messiah to earn salvation, and please God in material ways, such as by doing good works. Thus the promise of grace becomes muddied by the threat of divine wrath if you don't play your part in the traditional scheme of things.

A God capable of being pleased and displeased isn't a God of grace, since the essence of grace is unconditional love. There is a way to resolve this contradiction, but it can't be found by picking only the nice Jesus, or the not-nice Jesus, and twisting the evidence to support your choice. Fundamentalism, with its relentless emphasis on punishment for sins, chooses the not-nice Jesus, while liberal Christianity, which wants to be seen as totally benign, prefers the nice one. Since there are biblical verses that contradict both positions, neither is ultimately satisfactory. The only viable way to follow Jesus's teachings on love is to match them with your own level of consciousness.

Reality changes in different states of consciousness, and the same holds true for love. At lower levels of awareness our experience is dominated by the need to survive, and there are many threats to well-being. Love is experienced as temporary and far too weak to overcome the threat of violence. At this level of consciousness we feel victimized; we see no sign that God is watching, much less caring for us. In the midst of such experiences, divine grace seems a remote promise, at best. In order for grace to work, life must change, and for life to change, consciousness must change first.

This is why love provides the perfect litmus test. Each of us begins with an awareness that love has failed in many ways. We know we don't love our enemies; at times we doubt that we love our nearest and dearest as much as we should. We often act out of motives totally contrary to love, such as greed and selfishness. We look around and see little evidence that God loves us in the redemptive way that Jesus says he does. Evidence of inner growth is elusive and sometimes deceptive; we can pretend to be better than we really are or to see God in every cloud and flower. But Jesus's love is far more than a feeling of well-being and contentment. Its truth is connected to power. Its dawning is a radical experience and a sure sign that consciousness has been raised to the highest level.

Jesus's teachings are truly learned only when you *become* the teaching. There is already something deeply instinctive about love in all of us. Yet innate as love may seem, we didn't become love. We pick and choose whom to give our love to, but when the switch is turned off, we can be completely unloving. The lesson about divine love that Jesus taught is that love is so full of grace, it leads to transformation: it changes a person's whole being.

Grace Abounding

"You have heard that it was said, 'You shall love your neighbor and hate your enemy.' But I say to you, Love your enemies and pray for those who persecute you, so that you may be children of your Father in heaven; for he makes his sun rise on the evil and on the good, and sends rain on the righteous and on the unrighteous."

(Matthew 5:43–45)

This passage presents in capsule form everything that makes divine love so beautiful and yet so hard to live by. How can Jesus expect us to be like God and express love everywhere? The clue lies in the two images he chose: the sun and the rain. These are the basis of life, the very source of nourishment. Jesus is pointing us to our own source. There is a level of awareness inside everyone that is as steady as the sun and as life-giving as rain. This is pure Being, and without a connection to it, loving your enemy is impossible. For me, this passage is one of the clearest dividing lines between everyday consciousness and the higher state of consciousness that Jesus was teaching about. In another place, he says, "What is impossible for mortal is possible for God." Those words apply to loving your enemy, but instead of leaving it to God, we ourselves can rise to a level where love of everyone is spontaneous and natural.

Love Should Be Total

"You shall love the Lord your God with all your heart, and with all your soul, and with all your mind." This is the greatest and first commandment. And a second is like it: "You shall love your neighbor as yourself." On these two commandments hang all the law and the prophets.

(Matthew 22:37–40)

As beautiful and famous as this passage is, it's also one of the most divisive. Christians have split between the select few who can devote their whole lives to loving God and the vast majority who spend an occasional hour on Sunday loving him. But this is a false division, because the underlying assumption is that Jesus was talking about enormous amounts of time and effort. What he was actually talking about was wholeness. If your whole mind is given to loving God, a change occurs. The mind is no longer fragmented and distracted. It has found its source, which is God, and thus loving God is completely natural. To imply that this is a struggle is like saying that love of music is a struggle that leaves time for nothing else. The opposite is true. If you deeply love music or anything else, your love comes as naturally as breathing. This is what Jesus intended when it came to loving God.

Love Is Innocent

But when Jesus saw this, he was indignant and said to them, "Let the little children come to me; do not stop them; for it is to such as these that the kingdom of God belongs. Truly I tell you, whoever does not receive the kingdom of God as a little child will never enter it."

(Mark 10:14–15)

As if to underscore that love of God should be natural and spontaneous, Jesus compares it to the love of a child for his parents. By implication, everything we have learned about love as adults should be unlearned. Love that is selfish, conditional, and demanding cannot be turned into love for God. It must be transcended instead.

Live with Grace

> "But love your enemies, do good, and lend, expecting nothing in return. Your reward will be great, and you will be children of the Most High; for he is kind to the ungrateful and the wicked. Be merciful, just as your Father is merciful."
>
> *(Luke 6:35–36)*

Aware that people need to rise from their present state to a higher one, Jesus told them to live as if they were already there. Both aspects must be taken into account. It takes time to follow the spiritual path, gradually shifting one's beliefs and perceptions. Yet God supports any effort in the right direction, and therefore the best way to live at this very minute is with the knowledge that grace is real, even if that knowledge is not truly present without a shift in consciousness.

Love as I Love You

> "I give you a new commandment, that you love one another. Just as I have loved you, you also should love one another."
>
> *(John 13:34)*

The Old Testament already commands people to love one another, so what is new about this commandment lies in the words *just as I have loved you.* Jesus is emphasizing that it is important to love in God's fashion, not in the ordinary way. The Gnostics understood this, which is why their version reads, "Love your brother like your soul, guard him like the pupil of your eye." (Thomas 46) Only when another person is as close to you as your own soul is your love like Jesus's.

Love Earns Forgiveness

> Then turning toward the woman, he said to Simon, "Do you see this woman? I entered your house; you gave me no water for my feet, but she has bathed my feet with her tears and dried them with her hair. You gave me no kiss, but from the time I came in she has not stopped kissing my feet. You did not anoint my head with oil, but she has anointed my feet with ointment. Therefore, I tell you, her sins, which were many, have been forgiven; hence she has shown great love. But the one to whom little is forgiven, loves little."
>
> *(Luke 7:44–47)*

Jesus loved the humble because they did not set obstacles before his love. They served without ego, having no social status to lose. But the broader lesson here is that the ego blocks spiritual growth. Just as pride keeps some from greeting Jesus with love, it will keep them from greeting their own souls. Jesus also said on several occasions that he was sent to help those who most needed love, which included not only the poor and weak, but also the wicked. He compared himself to a doctor whose attention goes to the sick, since the well don't need healing.

Abide in Me

"If you abide in me, and my words abide in you, ask for whatever you wish, and it will be done for you. My Father is glorified by this, that you bear much fruit and be my disciples. As the Father has loved me, so I have loved you; abide in my love. If you keep my commandments, you will abide in my love, just as I have kept my Father's commandments and abide in his love. I have said these things to you so that my joy may be in you, and that your joy may be complete."

(John 15:7–11)

This is one of the longest and most eloquent passages in which Jesus describes divine love. Here he invites the reader to become part of Jesus, uniting with him in a love as intimate as the love of oneself. What is most moving, however, is the final part, when Jesus says that our love for him makes his joy complete. Too often we assume that Jesus is complete without us, that we need him but he doesn't need us. In a very human way Jesus says otherwise. His purpose is to fulfill God's will by bringing love to everyone, and the birth of a new humanity will ultimately make Christ fulfilled.

Nothing is more important, then, than rescuing Jesus's teaching of love for his sake. He doesn't make it easy, because the love he asks for is nearly impossible to achieve. We wonder in confusion about what kind of love God wants from us. Our only hope lies in finding out what divine love really is; the alternative has put us on a path filled with bloodshed and suffering.

Faith

The Jesus who speaks in the gospels seems obsessed by faith. He makes faith a condition for entering Heaven and escaping Hell. He heals the blind and the lame because they have faith. He declares that a mere speck of faith can work wonders. Moments of faith are among the most moving in the gospels:

> Then suddenly a woman who had been suffering from hemor-
> rhages for twelve years came up behind him and touched
> the fringe of his cloak, for she said to herself, "If I only touch
> his cloak, I will be made well." Jesus turned, and, seeing her,
> he said, "Take heart, daughter; your faith has made you well."
> And instantly the woman was made well.
>
> *(Matthew 9:20–22)*

No other virtue is more important than love. Faith was the requirement of a new religion that wanted to bond its members together. To be a Christian, you had to believe that Jesus was the Messiah and that he rose from the dead.

This is a thorny problem, because enlightenment isn't about faith. Nor is it about passing a loyalty test to prove that you are a devout follower. When Jesus tells someone whom he has just healed that their faith made the miracle possible, the implication is that God doesn't send miracles to the unfaithful.

Yet beyond the West the element of faith is usually a small part of hands-on healing. It is peculiarly Christian to put faith at the very center of religious life.

Why is that a difficulty for us? Because every time Jesus declares that faith is needed to achieve miracles, he doesn't focus on other spiritual techniques that could help a seeker on the path. In some ways faith is like a chimera, ever sought but never captured. Where is a specific, practical discipline akin to what Zen Buddhists are taught? The Church eventually devised spiritual disciplines of enormous rigor and complexity in the Middle Ages, but these weren't specified by Jesus.

Practical spiritual matters are shoved aside in the name of faith as the key to miracles and acceptance into the Kingdom of Heaven. The way out of this dilemma is to see that Jesus could be referring to faith as experienced in a higher state of consciousness. In other words, it takes only a speck of faith to move mountains if you are in God-consciousness, as Jesus was. Since he was attempting to raise his disciples to his own level, where miracles come naturally, I think this interpretation is correct. Before God-consciousness, faith is needed for many reasons: to keep you on the path, to keep you true to your vision, to confirm that God is on your side, and above all to give you the courage to step into the unknown. But in the end, when miracles dawn, faith in God becomes the same as faith in yourself.

Once we see Jesus as a teacher of enlightenment, faith changes its focus. You don't need to have faith in the Messiah or his mission. Instead, you have faith in the vision of higher consciousness. There are many times when such faith is needed, sometimes desperately; being on the path is lonely at times. Your experiences belong only to you, and as they ebb and flow, sometimes bringing you close to the soul and sometimes pulling you away, you need to trust that the goal is real. Jesus helps a great deal here, because no one in history was more secure in the reality of God and the Kingdom of Heaven to be found within ourselves.

Faith and the Light

"While you have the light, believe in the light, so that you may become children of light."

(*John 12:36*)

This is one of the most succinct and convincing things Jesus said about faith. Instead of saying "Believe in me," he refers his followers to his essence, which is the light of pure consciousness. In this way, the Book of John shifts focus away from the cult of Jesus to the deeper meaning of spirituality.

God Will Provide

"And can any of you by worrying add a single hour to your span of life? And why do you worry about clothing? Consider the lilies of the field, how they grow; they nei- ther toil nor spin, yet I tell you, even Solomon in all his glory was not clothed like one of these. But if God so clothes the grass of the field, which is alive today and tomorrow is thrown into the oven, will he not much more clothe you—you of little faith?"

(Matthew 6:27–30)

In the Sermon on the Mount, Jesus offers an idea so simple and rev- olutionary that it overturns everything we assume about existence. The idea is this: Let God take care of everything.

In this verse even the most basic necessity, clothing, is given over to God. But Jesus knew that the making of clothes requires work, so what could he mean by saying that God provides it? The crux of the matter is freedom. If you are free from the burden of toil, worry, and suffering, you can see that everything is provided by nature. Normally we think of ourselves as complex creatures, the exact opposite of lilies in a field, because our existence depends on struggle. In Jesus's eyes, this is a mistake.

Since we are closer to God in our ability to be aware, God

provides for us even more than he provides for plants and animals. But the way he provides isn't the same. Being conscious, we receive our sustenance through the mind. The physical world itself came from God's mind, and when we draw close to God, all of creation becomes part of us. In a very real sense we are clothed by divine glory. Without faith, this glory is hidden from sight. We feel that the world is separate from us and often hostile to our needs. It is necessary for Jesus, in his higher state of consciousness, to hold out a vision that will free us from this limited perception. Once that happens, we find ourselves basking effortlessly in glory, like the lilies of the field.

Believe in a Vision

"But strive first for the kingdom of God, and all these things will be given to you as well.

"So do not worry about tomorrow, for tomorrow will bring worries of its own. Today's trouble is enough for today."

(Matthew 6:33–34)

This passage, which directly follows the one previously given, tells Jesus's listeners how to gain the gifts of Providence. He has built up to this moment by declaring in the Sermon on the Mount that God provides all the necessities of life—food, clothing, shelter. His listeners, we can imagine, are waiting with bated breath to know how God does this, since this notion is so alien to their experience. Jesus has a lot to say on this subject, but the first thing is the most important: Work toward the highest vision. The Kingdom of God is an inner state. Instead of pointing to anything in the outer world, Jesus points here, where reality is created and therefore where it can be fulfilled.

The Door Will Open

"Ask, and it will be given to you; search, and you will find; knock, and the door will be opened for you. For everyone who asks receives, and everyone who searches finds, and for everyone who knocks, the door will be opened."

(Matthew 7:7–8)

There are many places in the gospels where I am not sure I hear the true voice of Jesus. Here, however, every note rings true, because Jesus is turning faith away from himself to the source, which is in everyone. Everyone who asks, receives. Every thought triggers a response; nothing is lost in the universe. Divine intelligence manifests whatever we can imagine.

Here Jesus underscores both the naturalness of spiritual growth and also its unlimited potential. But as the Sermon on the Mount reaches its final verses, he makes sure that his listeners realize the choice they face: "Everyone then who hears these words of mine and acts on them will be like a wise man who built his house on rock." (Matthew 7:24) The house is the self, and the rock on which it is built is pure, eternal, unchanging God-consciousness.

Nothing Will Be Impossible

When they came to the crowd, a man came to him, knelt before him, and said, "Lord, have mercy on my son, for he is an epileptic and he suffers terribly; he often falls into the fire and often into the water. And I brought him to your disciples, but they could not cure him." Jesus answered, "You faithless and perverse generation, how much longer must I be with you? How much longer must I put up with you? Bring him here to me." And Jesus rebuked the demon, and it came out of him, and the boy was cured instantly.

Then the disciples came to Jesus privately and said, "Why could we not cast it out?" He said to them, "Because of your little faith. For truly I tell you, if you have faith the size of a mustard seed, you will say to this mountain, 'Move from here to there,' and it will move; and nothing will be impossible for you."

(Matthew 17:14–20)

Jesus isn't in a typical mood. He is frustrated and disappointed in his followers. He has told them before that they have the power to heal, yet here they have failed. Now Jesus must confront yet again how different his level of consciousness is from that of everyone else. When it comes to miracles, Jesus seems to set the bar very low; all it takes is a speck of faith to perform a miracle. But at the same time, he sets the bar very high, because if we aren't performing miracles, we must not have even a speck of faith. I believe Jesus is exaggerating here to make his point unmistakably clear: Miracles begin with you. You must find the place inside yourself where nothing is impossible. The single word *faith* implies the whole spiritual path we must travel to arrive where Jesus already is. Jesus puts the matter concisely: "What is impossible with men is possible with God." (Luke 18:27)

Revelation and Redemption

Jesus was more than wise. He received direct knowledge from God, his source of secret wisdom. To this day, most Christians consider this connection unique. Only God's son could have been gifted with revelation in every word he spoke. Yet across many cultures, direct knowledge is a mark of higher consciousness. All thinking happens in the mind, yet the closer you get to the mind's source, the more your thoughts are like revelations. They no longer seem like "my" thoughts, the kind associated with everyday events and personal memories. Instead, you seem to tap into reality itself. Jesus spoke of divine reality, the revealed wisdom of the soul. The same experience is possible for anyone in higher consciousness. This is an aspect of intuition, and what is being revealed is the nature of the soul, or higher self.

Revelation was Jesus's primary means of communication. The disciples ask a question, and Jesus answers as God would. In the simplest terms, Jesus's mind was God's mind. Jesus didn't have to interpret anything; he was guided by pure truth. Needless to say, he provides a daunting model. Can we really expect our own thoughts to come directly from God?

Why not? Everyone knows what it is like to have an inspired moment; we've all been touched by ideas that seem to come from nowhere or by flashes of insight. These are glimpses of higher awareness. Or to put it another way, what would be the purpose of walking the spiritual path if your mind *didn't* change? Achieving insight and intuition is a reasonable expectation on the path, and Jesus intended to serve not as a supernatural phenomenon, but as an example of someone who has reached the goal.

Yes, there are times when Jesus makes it sound as if his position is unique. Only the Son of God knows what the Father wants to impart. Over and over, Jesus repeats the phrase *The Father and I are one.* But he also holds out the promise of revelation to his disciples. He makes them a promise: "And you will know the truth, and the truth will make you free." (John 8:32) Here he means revealed truth, the kind that arises directly from a real connection to God.

For Jesus, the truth wasn't abstract, it was practical; it set people free from every kind of bondage. Therefore, revelation is connected to redemption. Traditionally, redemption means finding religion and being rewarded by going to Heaven after you die. But being set free by the truth is a promise that can be fulfilled in the here and now. Freedom after death implies that there is no escape for the living, which is not what Jesus had in mind. A redeemed soul is one that has awakened. Dying isn't a requirement.

The soul journey begins in darkness, where truth is masked or misunderstood. The journey progresses by clearing away an obstacle to the truth every day. At times we make leaps into the light, great bounds that free us from the grip of an ignorant belief. More often, however, revelation proceeds by tiny steps, one insight at a time. Jesus talks about both aspects of the journey.

God Is Coming Soon

The time is fulfilled, and the kingdom of God is at hand.
Repent, and believe in the good news.

(Mark 1:15)

Jesus says "The kingdom of God is at hand" several times in the gospels, but this is the most dramatic instance, because he has just been baptized, gone into the wilderness, and returned to Galilee. His first words after being recognized as God's messenger tell people that he is on a rescue mission to save the world. Nor does this urgency apply only to persecuted Jews in the Roman Empire. "Near at hand" encourages each of us to find God within ourselves.

Redeem Yourself

> "Hearken to the word; understand knowledge; love life,
> and no one will persecute you, nor will anyone oppress
> you other than you yourselves."

(Apocryphon of Jesus 9:19–24)

Here I have made an exception to avoiding esoteric Gnostic writings because these verses are so apt and well expressed. The Gnostics were all about redeeming yourself, and here Jesus declares that the path is completely open through knowledge and love, the only obstacles being those that you raise yourself.

The same document eloquently goes on to say, "Do not make the kingdom of heaven a desert within you. Do not be proud because you are illumined by the light, but be to yourself as I am to you."

Death and New Life

> "Very truly, I tell you, unless a grain of wheat falls into
> the earth and dies, it remains just a single grain; but if it
> dies, it bears much fruit. Those who love their life lose it,
> and those who hate their life in this world will keep it for
> eternal life."

(John 12:24–25)

This passage is about transformation. Jesus tells his disciples that they must die to an old self in order to attain the new. As so often, he makes the teaching a matter of life and death, for it was Jesus's way to be as dramatic as possible. Here he says that if you are attached to your old way of being, death is inescapable. You must regard your present self as a seed. Once planted it will die, but from that extinction emerges the abundant reward of a new life, one that is beyond death.

Revelation Is Yours

Jesus said, "Whoever drinks from my mouth will become like me. I will be him, and the things that are hidden will be revealed to him."

(Thomas 83)

Because the Gnostic movement was based on personal revelation, it triggered suspicion from the official Church, which was threatened by revelations that could happen to anyone, regardless of religious infrastructure. Therefore, Gnostic beliefs like these were condemned. But seen in the light of higher consciousness, what Jesus says is undeniable: Anyone who reaches God-consciousness will experience revealed truth.

Nothing Can Be Hidden

"Nothing is covered up that will not be uncovered, and nothing secret that will not become known. Therefore whatever you have said in the dark will be heard in the light, and what you have whispered behind closed doors will be proclaimed from the housetops."

(Luke 12:1–3)

Jesus is warning his followers not to be hypocritical like the Pharisees, a frequent caution. But the broader meaning is more valuable. On the path, you confront things you would prefer to keep in the dark, not just secrets but every sort of negative energy. But hiding from fear, anger, shame, and guilt is pointless. In God's eyes, everything has been revealed already. When this truth is taken to heart, it becomes easier to reveal your secrets to yourself and in so doing to release them. This is one of the chief tools of redemption.

Forgiveness

"If your brother sins, you must rebuke the offender, and if there is repentance, you must forgive. And if the same person sins against you seven times a day, and turns back to you seven times and says, 'I repent,' you must forgive."

(Luke 17:3–4)

Christianity is burdened by some impossible expectations, and one of them is that God forgave all sins through Jesus. This all-at-once doctrine leaves us bewildered about how to react to the wrongs of others and to our own. Here Jesus makes forgiveness a process, which is more in keeping with spiritual growth: God will remove the effect of sin as many times as it takes before repentance (giving up the wrong act) finally sticks.

Know Thyself

Jesus said, "If a guide tells you, 'See, the kingdom of God is in the sky,' then the birds of the air will get there before you. If they tell you, 'It's in the sea,' the fish will get there before you.

"Rather, the kingdom is inside you and outside you at the same time. When you come to know yourself, then you will be known. You will realize then that it's you who are the sons of the living Father. But as long as you do not know yourself, you will live in poverty, and you will be that poverty."

(Thomas 62)

A Gnostic teaching like this one speaks to us more directly than much text in the four gospels. It's ironic, perhaps tragic, that seekers found the path to enlightenment so early (the Book of Thomas was written around the same time as the gospels), only to be told that they were wrong and the Church was right. But that happened long ago, and we are now free to consider that Jesus's words about knowing yourself are as genuine as anything else he spoke, perhaps more so.

The Good Shepherd

"If a shepherd has a hundred sheep, and one of them has gone astray, does he not leave the ninety-nine on the mountains and go in search of the one that went astray? And if he finds it, truly I tell you, he rejoices over it more than over the ninety-nine that never went astray. So it is not the will of your Father in heaven that one of these little ones should be lost."

(Matthew 18:12–14)

Setting aside the threat of punishment quoted on Judgment Day, Jesus uses the loving image of a shepherd who will rescue every stray sheep, overlooking no one. Now we see that redemption is an act born of love and caring.

Firsthand Knowledge

"You search the scriptures because you think that in them
you have eternal life; and it is they that testify on my behalf.
Yet you refuse to come to me to have life."

(John 5:39–40)

Jesus is making the point that secondhand knowledge is no substitute for direct knowledge. This passage could be read as a startling admonition not to read the gospels if you want to know the truth, but more significantly, Jesus is reinforcing his message that the Kingdom of God is within.

When Will the Kingdom Come?

His disciples asked Jesus, "When will the dead find peace?
When will the new world come?" Jesus replied, "What
you expect has already come, but you do not recognize it."

(Thomas 144)

This is a helpful reminder from the Gnostics that Judgment Day isn't a literal moment but an event that occurs within, at the level of the soul.

Jesus and the Self

Jesus devoted many teachings to the subject of the self, meaning the bundle of aspects we call "me." In this bundle are wrapped the ego, the personality, and the soul. They aren't neatly arranged into separate compartments but bleed confusingly into one another. Sometimes we feel close to the soul, sometimes very far away. More often we feel confused, unable to understand what the soul really is and what it wants.

Jesus spent a great deal of time clarifying this confusion. He said, "You do not understand me," in support of a deeper truth: "You do not know who you really are." By telling people who they really are, he delineates a new kind of human being, one who accepts that being one with God is our natural, higher state.

All great spiritual teachers want us to change, and the self is the vehicle for that change. Becoming new is an illusion unless the self you inhabit every day and recognize in the mirror starts to lose its old habits and conditioning.

The Beatitudes

When Jesus saw the crowds, he went up the mountain; and after he sat down, his disciples came to him. Then he began to speak, and taught them, saying:

"Blessed are the poor in spirit, for theirs is the kingdom of heaven.

"Blessed are those who mourn, for they will be comforted.

"Blessed are the meek, for they will inherit the earth.

"Blessed are those who hunger and thirst for righteousness, for they will be filled.

"Blessed are the merciful, for they will receive mercy.

"Blessed are the pure in heart, for they will see God.

"Blessed are the peacemakers, for they will be called children of God.

"Blessed are those who are persecuted for righteousness' sake, for theirs is the kingdom of heaven.

"Blessed are you when people revile you and persecute you and utter all kinds of evil against you falsely on my account. Rejoice and be glad, for your reward is great in heaven, for in the same way they persecuted the prophets who were before you."

(Matthew 5:1–12)

These are the most famous sayings from the Sermon on the Mount. They extol peace, humility, faith, mercy, and the other virtues of the righteous. It would be wrong, I think, to believe that Jesus was offering a litmus test for God's love. Too often we are tempted to compare ourselves to an ideal, only to fall short. That wasn't Jesus's intention. He was praising the virtuous while not condemning anyone else. Take this list as an inspiration for the kinds of transformations that occur on the path. Hold fast to this vision of the perfect Christian, but be realistic about your own qualities.

Being Selfless

He sat down, called the twelve, and said to them, "Whoever wants to be first must be last of all and servant of all."

(Mark 9:35)

The need to be selfless was paramount in Jesus's mind when he told people how to behave in the world. In modern terms, he was talking about breaking down the ego and its incessant self-importance. But his listeners in the first century lived in a world where masters stood high above servants and had absolute power over them, and in that time, Jesus's teaching was even more radical. However, his doctrine of "the last shall be first" wasn't an attempt to overturn the social order. It was aimed at revealing a deeper truth, that spirit has been put last in the world and deserves to be first.

God Values You

"Are not two sparrows sold for a penny? Yet not one of them will fall to the ground unperceived by your Father. And even the hairs of your head are all counted. So do not be afraid; you are of more value than many sparrows."

(Matthew 10:29–33)

When Jesus is being most reassuring, he is also often at his most baffling. Here he promises that God looks after the least detail in our lives, yet we all know (as his listeners surely did) what it feels like to be alone and completely unnoticed by God. To my mind, you cannot truly know that God is watching you unless you can see him. In other words, we need to know the mechanics whereby an invisible deity performs actions in the world that nurture and protect us. Such knowledge can be gained only by serious, diligent seeking—by opening a path to God-consciousness.

You Are the Light of the World

"You are the light of the world. A city built on a hill cannot be hidden. No one after lighting a lamp puts it under a bushel basket, but on the lamp stand, and it gives light to all in the house. In the same way, let your light shine before others, so that they may see your good works and give glory to your Father in heaven."

(Matthew 5:14–16)

Jesus constantly told his disciples that their essence was spirit. The Gnostics assigned great importance to this verse, which they restated even more emphatically: "Jesus said, 'If anyone asks, "Where do you come from?" tell them, "We came from the light, from the place where the light came into being of its own accord." If they ask, "Are you that light?" tell them, "We are its children, the chosen of the living Father." ' " (Thomas 143)

A Second Birth

Nicodemus said to him, "How can anyone be born after having grown old? Can one enter a second time into the mother's womb and be born?" Jesus answered, "Very truly, I tell you, no one can enter the kingdom of God without being born of water and Spirit. What is born of the flesh is flesh, and what is born of the Spirit is spirit. Do not be astonished that I said to you, 'You must be born from above.' The wind blows where it chooses, and you hear the sound of it, but you do not know where it comes from or where it goes. So it is with everyone who is born of the Spirit."

(John 3:3–8)

This passage is rich and beautifully expressed. It touches on the modern complaint against God that there is no evidence of his existence.

Jesus says that the evidence is subtle and comes at unexpected times. He compares the action of spirit to the wind, which everyone can hear but not everyone notices. Our second birth occurs on this subtle level, where perception shifts and a person suddenly notices that spirit has always been there, like the wind that has been taken for granted.

Old Wine in New Bottles

He also told them a parable: "No one tears a piece from a new garment and sews it on an old garment; otherwise the new will be torn, and the piece from the new will not match the old. And no one puts new wine into old wineskins; otherwise the new wine will burst the skins and will be spilled, and the skins will be destroyed. But new wine must be put into fresh wineskins. And no one after drinking old wine desires new wine, but says, 'The old is good.'"

(Luke 5:36–39)

This passage is stronger when the last phrase reads, "The old wine is better," as some versions have it. Jesus is referring to how many would rather stick with the old laws than to follow his new truth, but these words apply equally to belief in general. We resist giving up our old beliefs, so at best we try cautiously to blend the familiar with the new and unknown. Jesus argues that this won't work. He brings something radically new that must be accepted on its own terms.

Where the Heart Is

"Make purses for yourselves that do not wear out, an unfailing treasure in heaven, where no thief comes near and no moth destroys. For where your treasure is, there your heart will be also."

(Luke 12:33–34)

To me, this is one of Jesus's most astute commentaries on human nature. What you put your highest value on becomes, for all practical purposes, your conception of God.

Profit from God's Gifts

"For it is as if a man, going on a journey, summoned his slaves and entrusted his property to them; to one he gave five talents, to another two, to another one, to each according to his ability. Then he went away. The one who had received the five talents went off at once and traded with them, and made five more talents. In the same way, the one who had the two talents made two more talents. But the one who had received the one talent went off and dug a hole in the ground and hid his master's money.

"After a long time the master of those slaves came and settled accounts with them. Then the one who had received the five talents came forward, bringing five more talents, saying, 'Master, you handed over to me five talents; see, I have made five more talents.'

"His master said to him, 'Well done, good and trustworthy slave; you have been trustworthy in a few things, I will put you in charge of many things; enter into the joy of your master.'

"And the one with the two talents also came forward, saying, 'Master, you handed over to me two talents; see, I have made two more talents.'

"His master said to him. 'Well done, good and trust-worthy slave; you have been trustworthy in a few things, I will put you in charge of many things; enter into the joy of your master.'

"Then the one who had received the one talent also came forward, saying, 'Master, I knew that you were a harsh man, reaping where you did not sow, and gather-ing where you did not scatter seed; so I was afraid, and I went and hid your talent in the ground. Here you have what is yours.'

"But his master replied, 'You wicked and lazy slave! You knew, did you, that I reap where I did not sow, and gather where I did not scatter? Then you ought to have invested my money with the bankers, and on my return I would have received what was my own with interest. So take the talent from him, and give it to the one with the ten talents. For to all those who have, more will be given, and they will have an abundance; but from those who have nothing, even what they have will be taken away. As for this worthless slave, throw him into the outer darkness, where there will be weeping and gnashing of teeth.'"

(Matthew 25:14–30)

The meaning of this parable may be confusing, given all the times that Jesus speaks out against wealth. But here the coins that the master gives away are gifts from God, specifically the gift of knowl-edge that comes through Jesus. The moral is that once you hear the truth about God, which has been freely given to you, you can't bury it inside yourself but must act on it to make it grow.

As a Planted Seed Grows

"The kingdom of God is as if someone would scatter seed on the ground, and would sleep and rise night and day, and the seed would sprout and grow, he does not know how. The earth produces of itself, first the stalk, then the head, then the full grain in the head. But when the grain is ripe, at once he goes in with his sickle, because the harvest has come."

(Matthew 4:26–29)

This verse is about the way spirit grows inside you. It assures anyone on the path that enlightenment grows naturally. First the truth is planted in you, and there it grows until the day comes when the harvest, the state of God-consciousness, arrives. This is also a lesson in patience, since a seed grows slowly and out of sight.

Build on a Strong Foundation

"Why do you call me 'Lord, Lord,' and do not do what I tell you? I will show you what someone is like who comes to me, hears my words, and acts on them. That one is like a man building a house, who dug deeply and laid the foundation on rock; when a flood arose, the river burst against that house but could not shake it, because it had been well built. But the one who hears and does not act is like a man who built a house on the ground without a foundation. When the river burst against it, immediately it fell, and great was the ruin of that house."

(Luke 6:46–49)

Jesus speaks about needing to believe in him and his teachings, but remember that he is the light. Therefore, one can also say that the strong foundation that Jesus wants us to build is spirit itself, the light within. In many ways, he helped secure his disciples in the truth that they were of the light, just as he was.

Persistence on the Path

And he said to them, "Suppose one of you has a friend, and you go to him at midnight and say to him, 'Friend, lend me three loaves of bread; for a friend of mine has arrived, and I have nothing to set before him.' And he answers from within, 'Do not bother me; the door has already been locked, and my children are with me in bed; I cannot get up and give you anything.' I tell you, even though he will not get up and give him anything because he is his friend, at least because of his persistence he will get up and give him whatever he needs."

(Luke 11:5–8)

This is a good teaching to keep in mind when you feel that you aren't progressing on the path. You aren't doing anything wrong. Spirit grows spontaneously, in its own time. Have patience, and persist.

Be Humble

"When you are invited by someone to a wedding banquet, do not sit down at the place of honor, in case someone more distinguished than you has been invited by your host; and the host who invited both of you may come and say to you, 'Give this person your place,' and then in disgrace you would start to take the lowest place. But when you are invited, go and sit down at the lowest place, so that when your host comes, he may say to you, 'Friend, move up higher'; then you will be honored in the presence of all who sit at the table with you. For all who exalt themselves will be humbled, and those who humble themselves will be exalted."

(Luke 14: 8–11)

Jesus frequently speaks of humility being pleasing to God, and he prophesies that the humble will get their reward in the other world by being placed first. Here he takes a different tack, pointing out that if you make yourself important and deserving, someone will always come along who is more important and deserving. Yet I wonder if this view might not owe a lot to the writer of the gospel. The early Christians made a cult of humility because of the persecution they suffered. This is another one of those moments where we can't separate the true voice of Jesus from the voice that the writer of the gospel may have imposed on him.

God vs. Materialism

"No slave can serve two masters; for a slave will either hate the one and love the other, or be devoted to the one and despise the other. You cannot serve God and wealth."

(Luke 16:13)

Here's a Gnostic take on the same lesson: "Jesus said to them, 'It is impossible for a man to mount two horses or to stretch two bows. And it is impossible for a servant to serve two masters: otherwise, he will honor the one and treat the other with contempt.'" (Thomas 77) Notice that the emphasis here isn't on money or materialism, but on the question of allegiance. Whom do you align yourself with, God or the world? Jesus consistently taught that a person cannot divide his allegiance between these two realities.

The Downfall of Ego

"Two men went up to the temple to pray, one a Pharisee and the other a tax-collector. The Pharisee, standing by himself, was praying thus, 'God, I thank you that I am not like other people: thieves, rogues, adulterers, or even like this tax-collector. I fast twice a week; I give a tenth of all my income.' But the tax-collector, standing far off, would not even look up to heaven, but was beating his breast and saying, 'God, be merciful to me, a sinner!' I tell you, this man went down to his home justified rather than the other; for all who exalt themselves will be humbled, but all who humble themselves will be exalted."

(Luke 18:10–14)

Many people find it difficult to accept Jesus's teaching on being last. But it makes sense when we see what he is talking about in terms of the ego. When the ego dominates, the focus is on "I, me, mine" and therefore not on a higher reality. God can be found only where ego is not. To see this truth clearly is the first step to humility. The second is to act on Jesus's words and begin to depose the ego from its self-important status.

Accepting God's Offer

"Therefore I tell you, the kingdom of God will be taken away from you and given to a people that produces the fruits of the kingdom. . . ."

Once more Jesus spoke to them in parables, saying: "The kingdom of heaven may be compared to a king who gave a wedding banquet for his son. He sent his slaves to call those who had been invited to the wedding banquet, but they would not come. Again he sent other slaves, saying, 'Tell those who have been invited: Look, I have prepared my dinner, my oxen and my fat calves have been slaughtered, and everything is ready; come to the wedding banquet.'

"But they made light of it and went away, one to his farm, another to his business, while the rest seized his slaves, maltreated them, and killed them. The king was enraged. He sent his troops, destroyed those murderers, and burned their city.

"Then he said to his slaves, 'The wedding is ready, but those invited were not worthy.'"

(Matthew 21:43, 22:1–8)

This passage seems to cut both ways. God invites us into his reality, but if we don't accept his invitation, he punishes us. Too often, the punishment aspect has been emphasized. Just remember that existing outside God was punishment enough in Jesus's eyes, since sickness, age, and death are unavoidable in the material world.

The Blind and the Drunk

Jesus said, "I took my place in the midst of the world, and I appeared to them in the flesh. I found all of them drunk: I found none who were thirsty. My soul became sore for the sons of men. They are blind in their hearts, without sight. Empty they came into this world, and empty they seek to leave it. But for now they are drunk. When they shake off their wine, then they will repent."

(Thomas 70)

Although this teaching isn't found in the four gospels, it is one of the most poignant ways in which Jesus describes how ordinary people look through his eyes. Two additional passages from Thomas are similar, but even more blunt. In the first, when his disciples mention that there were twenty-four prophets in the Bible, Jesus replies, "You have left out the one living before you and speak only of the ones who are dead." (Thomas 75) The second passage could be taken as the first law of the Gnostics: "Jesus said, 'To those who are worthy of my mysteries I reveal my mysteries.'" (Thomas 76)

Meditation

The Christian seeker who wants to reach God is no different from the Buddhist. Both are directed into their own consciousness. Jesus, however, didn't come from a meditative tradition as Buddha did, and he placed his emphasis on prayer, faith, and knowledge. We have no scriptural evidence that he led his disciples in meditation practice. Worship was more in keeping with the Jewish tradition.

But to portray Jesus as traditional is to ignore the many times he rebukes people for thinking that they know where God is. He points out that God's location is mysterious, unfathomable by the mind alone. This is consistent with enlightenment, the transformation that isn't inner or outer but both at the same time, where the dividing line between reality "in here" and "out there" softens, blurs, and ultimately disappears. Here reality shifts from dualism to unity. As this happens, the relationship between inner events and outer ones changes radically. What is a miracle, after all, but the outer world obeying an intention of the mind?

Can we take Jesus to be a guru, a rabbi of the Ganges? That's certainly tempting, since the most detailed knowledge about inner transformation comes from India and predates Jesus by thousands of years. (Some scholars have traced links between Jesus's thoughts and the Vedic tradition, and there is much speculation that he might have visited India or come into contact with traders from there.) But it would be unfair to Easternize Jesus in this way. Jesus's teachings about the inner life remain vague. The gospel writers leave huge gaps in this area, and thanks to them and the early Church fathers, Christianity went on to emphasize worship over self-transformation, prayer over meditation, and faith over inner growth.

There is no equivalent in the New Testament of Psalm 46, "Be still, and know that I am God." It would be helpful if Jesus were as explicit as Psalm 37: "Be still before the Lord and wait patiently for him." One thing is certain, however. Some kind of revolution must occur inside for an ordinary person to enter the Kingdom of Heaven—Jesus is explicit about that. In the absence of meditation techniques that he might have taught, we can turn to the fact that for Jesus, being in God or with God isn't a state of action or even thought. Being is timeless. When Jesus says of himself, "Very truly, I tell you, before Abraham was, I am" (John 8:58), he is referring to his state of being. He isn't talking about a previous incarnation. If he were, he would say "before Abraham was, I was." Instead he uses the present tense, "I am," to denote an existence beyond time. It takes no great leap to believe that when Jesus told his followers to go inward, he wanted them to discover this state of being for themselves. Meditation, too, is founded on the basis of silent, unbounded, motionless being, as opposed to activity of the mind. Jesus teaches us what that is about, using terms like "One" and "All" to refer to an all-encompassing reality beyond the material world. Jesus calls this reality his source and identifies with it as his true essence.

I Am All

Jesus said, "I am the light that is above them all. I am the All. From me the All came forth, and in me the All manifests. Split open a piece of wood, and I am there. Lift up a stone, and you will find me beneath it."

(Thomas 78)

In the Gnostic Gospels, we find the most mystical Jesus, a teacher who goes beyond the Jesus found in the four gospels to wrap himself in ideas that cannot be grasped rationally. (The fact that the Book of Thomas is as old as the gospels should be kept in mind.) From the outset, the Gnostics realized that Jesus was trying to convey the ineffable. The All that he refers to here is Being itself, the central enigma that the Gnostics wanted to solve.

In the Christian tradition, contemplating the mystery of Christ was meditation: The mind was expected to delve deeply into mystery until truth revealed itself. The various Gnostic Gospels are full of conundrums and mystical declarations. I quote only a few examples here because so many of these gospels were set down centuries later. They almost certainly didn't originate with Jesus.

Eternal Treasure

> Jesus said, "The kingdom of God is like a merchant who finds a pearl mixed in with a consignment of merchandise. Being shrewd, he sold the rest of the merchandise so that he could buy the pearl for himself. So you, also, should seek God's unfailing and enduring treasure, which no moth comes near to devour and no worm to destroy."
>
> *(Thomas 83)*

This passage comes from the Gnostics. The mystical bent of the Gnostics led them to emphasize that God was hidden, secret, precious, and hard to find. Elsewhere in the Gospel of Thomas, the Kingdom of God is compared to a treasure hidden in a field by a farmer. Certainly it is hidden from the five senses and must be sought in the domain of the timeless.

A Hidden Mystery

> "All things have been handed over to me by my Father; and no one knows who the Son is except the Father, or

who the Father is except the Son and anyone to whom the
Son chooses to reveal him."

(Luke 10:22)

The Gnostics weren't straying from Jesus's own words when they
described spirit as a hidden mystery. The four gospels declare the
same thing, as in this passage.

The Mustard Seed

He put before them another parable: "The kingdom of
heaven is like a mustard seed that someone took and
sowed in his field; it is the smallest of all the seeds, but
when it has grown it is the greatest of shrubs and
becomes a tree, so that the birds of the air come and make
nests in its branches."

(Matthew 13:31–32)

Jesus uses the comparison of a mustard seed because it is nearly invisible but grows to a great size. I'm reminded of the Indian description
of Brahman, or universal Being, as "greater than the greatest and
smaller than the smallest." Jesus comes close to that in this passage.

Boundless and Timeless

"'I am the Alpha and the Omega,' says the Lord God,
who is and who was and who is to come, the Almighty."

(Revelation 1:8)

Within a few generations following Jesus's death, the mystical strain in Christianity had become powerful. His identification with God forced early Christians to contemplate the nature of God in order to understand Jesus himself. Thus in Revelation Christ returns as pure unbounded spirit, beyond time and space.

Overcoming Duality

> Jesus said, "When you make the two one, you will become the sons of men."
>
> *(Thomas 172)*

In this Gnostic verse, Jesus speaks explicitly about overcoming duality, but on many other occasions he addresses his listeners as someone who is in unity while they are not. In the first instance, Jesus is seeing his audience in an ideal light, as children of God. In the second instance, he is being more realistic. Everywhere in the New Testament he wrestles with the ideal and the practical. Like any good teacher, he wants his followers to be inspired without losing sight of life as it is lived.

Contemplation

Jesus gave his disciples many lessons to contemplate, and Christian thought continues to ponder his parables, sayings, and instructions. It's natural to follow the subject of meditation with contemplation, because the two go together. Both draw the seeker inward; both approach God on the plane of the mind. In meditation the mind is still, while in contemplation some idea or image expands and acquires deeper meanings. When you contemplate any spiritual teaching deeply enough, you are brought face-to-face with yourself and how you view the world.

And yet some of the time Jesus isn't contemplative. He's decisive. Some thorny problem is brought before him, and in short order he comes up with a brief, powerful, and memorable solution. Since he is the Messiah, no difficulty is beyond him; the temple high priests are foolishly lost by comparison. Jesus takes the attitude that once he has spoken, his words are not to be questioned.

It is on the basis of Jesus's answers that the early Christians drew their articles of belief. But there are other times in the gospels, far fewer in number, when Jesus poses questions himself, leaving his disciples to find the answer. He draws them into contemplation. And he contemplates on his own. We find him musing on his fate, for instance. He was aware of the sacrifice God would ask him to make long before events unfolded. The nearness of impending death became the subject of his deepest contemplation, most famously in the garden of Gethsemane just before Judas betrayed him to the Romans.

But contemplation of death wasn't what Jesus asked of others. Instead, he wanted them to contemplate God and the spiritual life. He wanted their minds to turn in the direction of the soul, which is where the line between meditation and contemplation blurs. Commonly we hear someone say, "I'll have to meditate on it," meaning that some idea or situation needs deeper reflection. This is also what the church means by meditation. The faithful are asked to meditate on the Crucifixion or on their own sins, on the promise of salvation or the Holy Spirit. Shouldn't this really be called contemplation? Perhaps the distinction doesn't need to be drawn too strictly. In deep contemplation, the idea or image you begin with leads to silence.

At this point I'd like to encourage you to undertake a shift in the way you read the material in the next few pages. Rather than just give you an intellectual understanding of contemplation, I'd like you to taste contemplation as an experience. Contemplation is a fascinating process that everyone needs to experience on the spiritual path, since it allows expansion of the mind. Contemplation begins with a thought that attracts you; as you consider it, its attraction expands and deepens. As it does, a feeling emerges from the idea or image that you began with. In the case of the idea of God's love, for example, the feeling of being loved will emerge. New feelings are also discovered. If you contemplate the Crucifixion, for example, the feeling might be sorrow, awe, wonder, grief, or simply the sensation of being present at a mysterious event.

Whatever the feeling, if you stay with it long enough, a change occurs. By subtle degrees the feeling becomes impersonal. It is no longer suffused with personal associations and memories. Something may be glimpsed behind the screen of thought, a sense that you have entered a deeper reality. Next, you may sense a hidden presence that cannot be described but can still be felt. Grief may give way to joy. Awe may give way to ecstasy, wonder to a sense of lightness or floating. These changes signal the approach of the soul. They transform an everyday idea into something rarefied and pure.

This process is spontaneous and takes place according to its own timing. As you read the verses that follow, sit for a few minutes to reflect on them, letting your mind go where it will. (Don't read more than one or two verses at a time; you will want to get the full effect of each one.) Don't try to force the words to create an immediate shift inside. You may feel a little inspired but nothing more, or perhaps not inspired but something altogether different. Whatever you feel, let the words stay with you for a while. Let them incubate, and be patient. A result will come in time.

For this section I've selected a range of sayings from Jesus, some beautiful, others intriguing, mysterious, or even inexplicable. But each one can be used as a doorway for entering the deeper reality Jesus consistently pointed to. I'd also like to suggest that any of Jesus's words quoted in this book can be used for contemplation. (Note: Since the following passages are for your own contemplation, I have omitted commentary.)

On Mercy

"[God] is kind to the ungrateful and the wicked. Be merciful, just as your Father is merciful."

(Luke 6:35–36)

On Charity

"Whenever you give alms, do not sound a trumpet before you, as the hypocrites do in the synagogues and in the streets, so that they may be praised by others. Truly I tell you, they have received their reward. But when you give alms, do not let your left hand know what your right hand is doing, so that your alms may be done in secret; and your Father who sees in secret will reward you."

(Matthew 6:1–4)

On Being Judgmental

"Why do you see the speck in your neighbor's eye, but do not notice the log in your own eye? Or how can you say to your neighbor, 'Friend, let me take out the speck in your eye,' when you yourself do not see the log in your own eye? You hypocrite, first take the log out of your own eye, and then you will see clearly to take the speck out of your neighbor's eye."

(Luke 6:41–42)

On Good and Evil

"No good tree bears bad fruit, nor again does a bad tree bear good fruit; for each tree is known by its own fruit. Figs are not gathered from thorns, nor are grapes picked from a bramble bush. The good person out of the good treasure of the heart produces good, and the evil person out of evil treasure produces evil; for it is out of the abundance of the heart that the mouth speaks."

(Luke 6:43–45)

On Providence

"Therefore I tell you, do not worry about your life, what you will eat or what you will drink, or about your body, what you will wear. Is not life more than food, and the body more than clothing? Look at the birds of the air; they neither sow nor reap nor gather grain into barns, and yet your heavenly Father feeds them. Are you not of more value than they?"

(Matthew 6:25–26)

Not by Bread Alone

"It is written, 'One does not live by bread alone, but by every word that comes from the mouth of God.'"

(Matthew 4:4)

What Is Real?

"It is the spirit that gives life; the flesh is useless. The words that I have spoken to you are spirit and life. But among you there are some who do not believe."

(John 6:63–64)

Care of the Soul

Then he told this parable: "A man had a fig tree planted in his vineyard; and he came looking for fruit on it and found none. So he said to the gardener, 'See here! For three years I have come looking for fruit on this fig tree, and still I find none. Cut it down! Why should it be wasting the soil?' He replied, 'Sir, let it alone for one more year, until I dig round it and put manure on it. If it bears fruit next year, well and good; but if not, you can cut it down.'"

(Luke 13:6–9)

Hasten to God

"Hasten to be saved without being urged! Be eager of your own accord, and if you can, arrive even before me, for that will cause your Father to love you."

(Apocryphon of Jesus 49)

On Materialism

And he said to them, "Take care! Be on your guard against all kinds of greed; for one's life does not consist in the abundance of possessions."

(Luke 12:15)

Using the Power

"Cure the sick, raise the dead, cleanse the lepers, cast out demons. You received without payment; give without payment. Take no gold, or silver, or copper in your belts, no bag for your journey, or two tunics, or sandals, or a staff; for laborers deserve their food.

"Whatever town or village you enter, find out who in it is worthy, and stay there until you leave. As you enter the house, greet it. If the house is worthy, let your peace come upon it; but if it is not worthy, let your peace return to you."

(Matthew 10:8–13)

The Water of Life

"Everyone who drinks of this water will be thirsty again, but those who drink of the water that I will give them will never be thirsty. The water that I will give will become in them a spring of water gushing up to eternal life."

(John 4:13–14)

The Voice of Truth

Pilate asked him, "So you are a king?" Jesus answered, "You say that I am a king. For this I was born, and for this I came into the world, to testify to the truth. Every-one who belongs to the truth listens to my voice."

(John 18:37)

You Will Do Greater

"Very truly, I tell you, the one who believes in me will also do the works that I do and, in fact, will do greater works than these. . . . If in my name you ask for any-thing, I will do it."

(John 14:12–14)

Prayer

Jesus prays frequently in the four gospels, addressing God personally as his father. Jesus tells his followers that they, too, can ask God for anything, and their prayers will be answered. Since it's a universal experience that many prayers go unanswered, Christians have been confused ever since. How literally can they take the promises Jesus made? Clearly he considers prayer a powerful thing, for several reasons. It serves as a way for ordinary people to tell God what they want. It affirms that God is master of the world and ruler of destiny. It opens the heart to worship and gratitude, praising God for his goodness and thanking him for the fruits he bestows.

Christians use prayer for all these things today, yet in an age of doubt, it's difficult to believe that prayer can achieve as much as Jesus claims. For him, prayer has no limits. Whether one prays to the Father or the Son, Jesus is absolute that no request will be denied. The single most famous prayer in the Bible, the Lord's Prayer, asks God for the necessities of life ("our daily bread"), a pure existence ("lead us not into temptation"), protection from danger ("deliver us from evil"), and a blanket pardon ("forgive us our trespasses"). In other words, the Lord's Prayer asks God for Heaven on earth. That God could grant this seems idealistic to the point of impossibility. Our world may have progressed since the first century, but the Lord's Prayer hasn't delivered Heaven on this material plane.

The one thing that can make the Lord's Prayer real is enlightenment. A person in God-consciousness would address the Father exactly as Jesus does. Jesus offers many eloquent prayers, but he speaks of the mechanics of prayer only a few times. In the gospels, Jesus comes back to the theme of "ask and you shall receive" time and again. If he did the same in life, his followers must have pointed out that they asked God for many things that never came about. Jesus must have had an answer, even though it isn't recorded in scripture. We are left to surmise how he would have answered based on his level of consciousness.

Prayer changes as you progress on the spiritual path, becoming more powerful on the basis of consciousness. God doesn't grant or deny prayers, nor does he hear some and turn a deaf ear to others. These are appearances seen from your particular level of awareness. Thus Jesus put the blame for unanswered prayers on the one who prays rather than on God. Instead of being discouraged, we need to accept this as a statement of fact.

Prayer isn't magic. It's applied consciousness. You cannot expect God to fulfill your request unless there is an intimate connection with spirit. Jesus was keenly aware of this, since he lived from the source of reality and therefore could change reality at will. The closer our connection with God, the greater our spiritual power.

Pray to Be Worthy

"Be on guard so that your hearts are not weighed down with dissipation and drunkenness and the worries of this life, and that day does not catch you unexpectedly, like a trap. For it will come upon all who live on the face of the whole earth. Be alert at all times, praying that you may be counted worthy to escape all these things that will take place, and to stand before the Son of Man."

(Luke 21:34–36)

When he refers to "the things that will take place," Jesus was speaking about the arrival of Heaven on earth. In the gospels, he makes it seem that this apocalyptic event is imminent, and early Christians took him literally. But we don't know why Jesus made such a prediction or even if he did. Literalism has always had to fight against symbolism in spiritual matters.

I believe that in this passage Jesus is giving his followers a way to approach spirit in everyday life—in other words, an attitude toward their own growth. "Being alert at all times" means being self-aware, which in Buddhism is known as "mindfulness." Jesus goes so far as to provide detailed instructions about what this entails, which can be summarized as follows: Remember who you really are, live to be worthy of God, pray so that you will be connected to him. This points to prayer as a means to remain alert to matters of spiritual importance.

The Intimacy of Prayer

"And whenever you pray, do not be like the hypocrites; for they love to stand and pray in the synagogues and at the street corners, so that they may be seen by others. Truly I tell you, they have received their reward. But whenever you pray, go into your room and shut the door and pray to your Father who is in secret; and your Father who sees in secret will reward you."

(Matthew 6:5–6)

At one level this passage speaks for itself. Jesus advises that prayer should be a private communion, not a public show. But what does Jesus mean by the phrase *pray to your Father who is in secret?* This is ambiguous, to say the least, because Jesus's listeners assumed that God wasn't secret. After all, they went to a public place, the synagogue, to worship a public God. But Jesus says that God is hidden, implying that he must be sought for and that our relationship to God has a mysterious aspect.

Knowledge Comes to the Innocent

At that time Jesus said, "I thank you, Father, Lord of
heaven and earth, because you have hidden these things
from the wise and the intelligent and have revealed them
to infants; yes, Father, for such was your gracious will."

(Matthew 11: 25–26)

Jesus often implies that what God wants to communicate doesn't
come through the mind as thoughts, but here he says it explicitly.
What kind of knowledge has been hidden from the wise and the
intelligent, and why does Jesus praise God for that? The conventional answer is that he wants his followers to understand that only
by believing in him is God revealed. But the broader implication is
that the spirit communicates not through words but through direct
experience. Infants learn about life by experiencing it, yet people
believe they can learn about God secondhand, through authorities
and scriptures. Jesus is underscoring the need to be in the presence
of spirit yourself and to be affected by it personally.

God Already Knows

"When you are praying, do not heap up empty phrases as
the Gentiles do; for they think that they will be heard
because of their many words. Do not be like them, for
your Father knows what you need before you ask him."

(Matthew 6:7–8)

On the surface, Jesus is telling his followers to be sincere in their
prayers, to speak from the heart instead of using rhetoric. But God

already knows what you want, why pray in the first place? This isn't a new question, and various answers have been given. God needs to know that you want his help. It does a person good to ask in humility, to bow before the Divine. It clarifies the mind to ask specifically for what you want God to do. All these answers, and others besides, evade the central question of why an omniscient God needs to be told anything. Being all-knowing, God should run the world without needing a human nudge.

I believe Jesus valued prayer as a process of inner growth. He doesn't say that instead of relying on God implicitly, you should come to God in prayer. Yet if we take the position that Jesus was a teacher of enlightenment, prayer is in service of that end. When you pray to an omniscient God, you are linking your awareness to pure awareness. This connection becomes more intimate as you progress on the path.

In the beginning you may offer love to God because you feel a genuine love for God or perhaps because you know that prayers should contain love. This love will wax and wane, as it does in every relationship, but in time love deepens, and it reveals mysteries never contemplated at the beginning. Prayer is a way to keep this process alive and to monitor it as you go.

When you express yourself in a relationship, you want a response. Silence implies that the relationship is blocked; constant silence implies that it is over. So prayer is also a test to see if God is listening, if your relationship to spirit has any energy running through it.

Pray with Faith

"Whatever you ask for in prayer with faith, you will receive."

(Matthew 21:22)

This is perhaps the simplest expression of a teaching that Jesus repeats often. One must have faith. Other translations of this short verse say, "Believe that you will receive." So for centuries the act of prayer has had a hidden component: a litmus test for faith. It's very hard to utter a prayer without also feeling a twinge of guilt and doubt. Do I have enough faith? What's wrong with me if my prayer isn't answered? Obeying this injunction depends, as everything does, on your level of consciousness. At lower levels, one begs for help. At the highest level, a prayer is no different from any other thought, because all thoughts bring about a result. In between lies a wide range of possibilities. Jesus certainly knew that, but he tells us to believe that our prayers will come true.

This is a valuable teaching at any level of consciousness. Assume that Jesus is telling the truth, that prayer is meant to be answered. If so, then praying can bring only one or two results: Either things go normally and your prayer brings a response, or you face some obstacle or resistance that blocks a response. Obstacles and resistance exist in consciousness and therefore can be cleared away. Instead of being a litmus test for faith, prayer shows you what you need to do on the spiritual path is to open the channels of communication. The help that Jesus offers is to assure us that communication is never cut off; it is only temporarily blocked.

Karma—Reaping and Sowing

Finding out how much Jesus has to say about Karma was one of my great surprises in writing this book. The primary tenet of Karma is that every action works like a seed that sprouts and brings fruit in the form of a result. Jesus isn't identified with such an Eastern concept, yet he famously said, "As you sow, so shall you reap." All he lacked was the word *Karma,* because throughout the four gospels we are told that every action has a consequence, either here or in Heaven.

Karma is important on the spiritual path, and knowing how to act and why is important in all religions. In Jesus's time the laws of Moses indicated that certain acts were sins. The list of acts disagreeable to God was long, and since God was irascible and fickle, trying to avoid sin was a complex business. It took a busy hierarchy of priests to determine right from wrong. The Old Testament Book of Leviticus prescribed hundreds of duties and laid down innumerable rules for the virtuous Jewish life.

Jesus was well aware of the law, and sometimes he simply tells people to obey it. But at other times he wants to free his followers from the law, to put them directly in contact with why an action is right or wrong. Instead of leaving the matter to priests, whom he distrusted thoroughly, or to a rigid set of rules, he appealed to his followers at the level of heart, mind, and soul.

This kind of freedom to determine your own actions was new and radical. No wonder the Jesus we meet in the gospels sometimes lapses into being the traditional rabbi. But since freedom is the goal of the spiritual path, it's important to see where Jesus offers it. The law of Karma was binding as he taught it—every action led to a result with moral weight—but God held the key for escaping that bondage.

Jesus speaks about how actions earn favor with God, which we can translate to mean how actions advance spiritual growth. Jesus wanted his followers to evolve, to reach awareness of the Kingdom of God within. Although Jesus often sounds absolute, simplifying Karma into a matter of avoiding sin and obeying the law, the gospels still present a good deal of wisdom about how to live on the spiritual path. His version of Karma can be summarized as follows:

Every action leads to a result.

Good actions have good results, bad actions bad results.

Every action is seen and weighed. Nothing can be hidden or kept secret.

If your actions are good, you will grow spiritually.

As you grow, your thoughts and wishes will manifest in the material world. Karma operates faster and more consciously.

God's intention is to make your actions turn out for the best. His ultimate concern is to bring you into the Kingdom, where the soul is freed from the law of Karma.

The Golden Rule

"Is there anyone among you who, if your child asks for bread, will give a stone? Or if the child asks for a fish, will give a snake? If you, then, who are evil, know how to give good gifts to your children, how much more will your Father in heaven give good things to those who ask him! In everything do to others as you would have them do to you."

(Matthew 7:9–12)

Everyone knows the Golden Rule, but this is a statement about Karma, not just about how to act morally toward other people.

Certainly Jesus intended to make the latter point: Treating others as you want to be treated is part of his larger teaching to love others as you love yourself. But Jesus implies something deeper, that when you follow the Golden Rule, you are acting as God does. What makes it hard to treat others the way we want to be treated is that others may be the cause of misery, pain, and injustice. But Jesus points out that each of us is evil in his or her own way, in that we all commit wrong-doing, and yet God provides abundantly and with love. This is a compelling description of how someone acts in God-consciousness.

If you look even deeper, however, this passage is about grace. Karma gives back exactly what you deserve, but God doesn't. He gives without regard to good and evil, and that is a mark of grace. If you contemplate the Golden Rule, it turns out to be an injunction to live by grace rather than by what you think other people deserve.

Judge Not

"Do not judge, so that you may not be judged. For with the judgment you make you will be judged, and the measure you give will be the measure you get."

(Matthew 7:1–2)

When Jesus tells his followers that they should show mercy to everyone and not judge them, he cites two principal reasons. The first is that everyone has done wrong at one time or another and could be judged in kind (as expressed by John 8:7 when a crowd is about to stone an adulterous woman: "Let anyone among you who is without sin be the first to throw a stone at her"). The second reason is karmic, as stated above: The way you judge others will be visited on your own actions. If you are harsh toward others, your wrongs will be judged harshly, but if you are merciful toward others, your wrongs will be treated mercifully.

Clearly Jesus believed that every action had consequences that often were not immediately apparent, which is the key to Karma. If we experienced the immediate result of our actions, there would be no need of a divine judge to settle accounts later on. When will we be judged? How heavy is each wrong, weighing the slight ones with the serious ones? Can a bad action be erased by another good one? Jesus cuts through all these complicated issues by saying, without equivocation, Don't judge. The ego cannot help but judge, so by implication Jesus is pointing toward a level of awareness that is acceptable only at the level of the soul. As we move toward higher consciousness, our need to rigidly judge right and wrong begins to soften. We no longer have to blame; we stop thinking in terms of sin and punishment. This is all consistent with his emphasis on love and forgiveness.

Give Good Measure

"Forgive, and you will be forgiven; give, and it will be given to you. A good measure, pressed down, shaken together, running over, will be put into your lap; for the measure you give will be the measure you get back."

(Luke 6:37–38)

Jesus used practical, homey comparisons when he taught. His listeners went to market every day for their food. They wanted good measure from the grain merchant, so it was easy to understand Jesus's teaching that if you give good measure, you will receive good measure. And the rule that operated in the marketplace also applied to God. Generosity of spirit is rewarded in kind.

Like Attracts Like

"Whatever house you enter, first say, 'Peace to this house!'
And if anyone is there who shares in peace, your peace will
rest on that person; but if not, it will return to you."

(Luke 10:5–6)

Traditional Christians usually don't like to concede that Jesus had
Eastern ideas, overlooking the possibility that spiritual truths can't
be restricted by time and place. Here Jesus expands on the doctrine
of Karma by saying that like attracts like. The ability to receive any
spiritual teaching depends on your level of awareness.

God Draws You to Me

"It is written in the prophets, 'And they shall all be taught
by God.' Everyone who has heard and learned from the
Father comes to me. Not that anyone has seen the Father
except the one who is from God; he has seen the Father."

(John 6:45–46)

God makes himself known to people, and then they are drawn to
Jesus, because his truth resonates with what they already know. This
is the karmic principle of like being attracted to like, discussed in
the preceding passage.

Jesus goes on to say that complete knowledge of God comes
only to someone who has seen God, and that is possible only
through union with him. To devout Christians, this passage is about
worshipping Christ as the way to God, but the implications for

God-consciousness are just as strong. Pure spirit is drawing us up to its level. Jesus also calls this "passing from death to life."

Give Away Your Possessions

"Or what king, going out to wage war against another king, will not sit down first and consider whether he is able with ten thousand to oppose the one who comes against him with twenty thousand? If he cannot, then, while the other is still far away, he sends a delegation and asks for the terms of peace. So, therefore, none of you can become my disciple if you do not give up all your possessions."

(Luke 14:31–33)

This is one of several places where Jesus commands his disciples to give up material things. Having blessed the poor, he wants his disciples to imitate the poor. Needless to say, this commandment has caused much discomfort over the centuries. It is one of the reasons that Jesus's teachings seem so incompatible with a life in the material world. Following the example of Saint Francis of Assisi, some devout Christians have given away all their possessions and literally embraced the teaching, whereas others have seen it as being about renunciation that is spiritual rather than material. The result is an uneasy compromise.

I chose this parable because it seems to offer clarification. The king who looks ahead to the battle and sees that his enemy is twice as strong in arms uses good judgment by sending a peace envoy so that he doesn't face certain defeat. By implication, each of us can see that when death comes, our worldly ambitions will have been tested once and for all. If we anticipate this moment, we should make peace with God in advance. It is wiser to turn toward the soul early rather than late.

Those Who Live by the Sword

Jesus said to him, "Friend, do what you are here to do." Then they came and laid hands on Jesus and arrested him. Suddenly, one of those with Jesus put his hand on his sword, drew it, and struck the slave of the high priest, cutting off his ear. Then Jesus said to him, "Put your sword back into its place; for all who take the sword will perish by the sword. Do you think that I cannot appeal to my Father, and he will at once send me more than twelve legions of angels?"

(Matthew 26:50–53)

In a sense, all of us live by the sword. We support armies and the police to protect us. We assume that it takes force to repel force. Jesus knew that the world worked this way, but he is declaring violence to be part of a cycle of life and death that never ends. He, on the other hand, has escaped the cycle. Jesus functions on the level of angels, next to God. The Passion is full of such symbolism that needs to be read in the light of higher consciousness and not simply the tragedy of supreme goodness condemned to die. All the violence in Jesus's life served the purpose of a higher teaching, that physical life, even at its most cruel, can be transcended.

Freedom from Karma

"For my yoke is easy, and my burden is light."

(Matthew 11:30)

Jesus is promising his followers that there is no toil in Heaven. But the deeper implication is that in higher consciousness, the burden of Karma no longer exists. This is his own experience, underscored by the fact that the English word *yoke* comes from the same root word as *yoga,* or "union with God."

The World as Illusion

Not all spiritual teachers are opposed to materialism, but Jesus was. He spoke out against worldliness in all its forms. The priests were castigated for their hypocrisy and love of public importance. The rich and powerful were scorned as unworthy of God. These criticisms were reinforced by praising the lowliest people in society, the poor and meek. There seems to be no escape clause here. If we feel uncomfortable being so attached to our own money, possessions, and status, the Jesus we meet in the gospels wants us to be uncomfortable.

But why? We assume that he had a moral aversion to money and power, and certainly when he says, "Give to Caesar the things that are Caesar's, and give to God the things that are God's" (Matthew 22:21), Jesus is divorcing himself from the world because it has nothing to do with his spiritual mission. Yet he seems to be contradicting this stance when he says, "For to those who have, more will be given, and they will have an abundance." (Matthew 13:12)

To resolve such contradictions, we need to look to Jesus's teaching that the world itself is an illusion. If material things are a dream, it makes sense to pay them no heed. When Jesus rails against "the deceitfulness of riches," the reason is that consciousness itself is being deceived. The mind is pulled away from spiritual goals by mistaking money, possessions, and status as real. That's why Jesus calls possessions a "consolation." Having missed the real prize, the Kingdom of God, one must settle for the material world, the consolation prize.

Separating illusion from reality doesn't usually happen all at once. What we experience as reality changes in different stages of consciousness. For those few who decide to renounce the world completely, it's possible to leap directly toward the goal. But even then there is no guarantee that perception has actually shifted. A person may enter a monastery because the Church deems that a holy life. But if old perceptions get dragged through the door, the monastery holds the same traps as the material world: ego.

Jesus wanted his disciples to come into union with God. Any other life was steeped in illusion. Ego keeps that illusion strong because "I, me, and mine" is so rooted in worldly affairs. The most worthwhile life is spent discovering your spiritual core and building your existence on it. If you do that, you will be first in the eyes of God even if you are last in the eyes of the world.

Avoiding the World

> So his brothers said to him, "Leave here and go to Judea so that your disciples also may see the works you are doing; for no one who wants to be widely known acts in secret. If you do these things, show yourself to the world."(For not even his brothers believed in him.)
>
> Jesus said to them, "My time has not yet come, but your time is always here. The world cannot hate you, but it hates me because I testify against it that its works are evil. . . ."
>
> *(John 7:3–7)*

This is one of Jesus's harshest denunciations of the world. The context for this passage is that he was refusing to go to Jerusalem for a Jewish feast day because he knew that there were those who wanted to kill him there. The evil of the world is a subject Jesus returns to frequently, contrasting it with the goodness of God's world. But we need to keep in mind that he is talking to skeptics who believe completely in the world. There was good reason to use the strongest words possible to shake them out of their beliefs.

The Falseness of Life

"Do not think that I have come to bring peace to the earth; I have not come to bring peace, but a sword. For I have come to set a man against his father, and a daughter against her mother . . . one's foes will be members of one's own household. Whoever loves father or mother more than me is not worthy of me; and whoever loves son or daughter more than me is not worthy of me. . . . Those who find their life will lose it, and those who lose their life for my sake will find it."

(Matthew 10:34–39)

Here, Jesus labels even the most cherished aspect of material life as false. We may find it easy to side with him against the rich and powerful, but here Jesus sides against the family itself! Not even this aspect of material life is worthwhile, compared to the life that lies ahead on the spiritual path. (So much for "family values"!)

Seeing What Is Real

"No one after lighting a lamp puts it in a cellar, but on the lamp stand so that those who enter may see the light. Your eye is the lamp of your body. If your eye is healthy, your whole body is full of light; but if it is not healthy, your body is full of darkness. Therefore consider whether the light in you is not darkness. If then your whole body is full of light, with no part of it in darkness, it will be as full of light as when a lamp gives you light with its rays."

(Luke 11:33–35)

This passage is about perception. If you can perceive the light within, you will gain its fullness. But if you are blind to it, you will have none. The reality you find yourself in depends on you. The light is God's reality, the dark is the absence of God. As ever, Jesus urges his listeners to seek the light.

Connect to the Source

"I am the true vine, and my Father is the vine-grower. He removes every branch in me that bears no fruit. Every branch that bears fruit he prunes to make it bear more fruit. You have already been cleansed by the word that I have spoken to you. Abide in me as I abide in you. Just as the branch cannot bear fruit by itself unless it abides in the vine, neither can you unless you abide in me. I am the vine, you are the branches. Those who abide in me and I in them bear much fruit, because apart from me you can do nothing."

(John 15:1–5)

Jesus wanted to share the unity he experienced with God, and therefore he often used the phrase *abide in me*. The parable of the grapevine (one of the rare times that the Book of John quotes a parable) elaborates on the point. Jesus declares that being cut off from God is sterile and fruitless. The sap that nourishes the vine and causes it to bear fruit is God, the source of life. By implication, the only life that escapes death is one that connects back to its ultimate source.

Spirit Is Eternal

"From the fig tree learn its lesson: as soon as its branch becomes tender and puts forth its leaves, you know that summer is near. So also, when you see all these things, you know that he is near, at the very gates. Truly I tell you, this generation will not pass away until all these things have taken place. Heaven and earth will pass away, but my words will not pass away."

(Matthew 24:32–35)

This is one of many passages where Jesus tells his followers that redemption is an urgent matter. Just as the first buds of the fig tree foretell the height of summer, the nearness of God signals a new world. As a literal prophecy, this one was fallible. Jesus may have seen himself as the harbinger of God on earth, but high summer has yet to arrive. But the greater urgency involves finding eternal reality rather than focusing on the transient world. Jesus is pressing the disciples to move swiftly onto the spiritual path if they want to outpace illusion.

Love It or Lose It?

"Those who love their life lose it, and those who hate their life in this world will keep it for eternal life."

(John 12:25)

Here Jesus is at his most uncompromising. The dichotomy between life and death is as sharp as a knife blade. But I tend to see such moments of absolutism as rhetorical. Jesus wants to shock his listeners into seeing that they have not properly placed their values: Worldly attachment leads to death; spiritual awakening leads to freedom and eternal life.

Where I Come From

Jesus answered, "Even if I testify on my own behalf, my testimony is valid because I know where I have come from and where I am going, but you do not know where I come from or where I am going. You judge by human standards; I judge no one."

(John 8:14–15)

Here Jesus is defending himself before the priests, who object that he calls himself the Messiah. The older versions of the Bible use the poetic phrase *You judge by the flesh* instead of the modern but awkward *You judge by human standards*. The older wording helps to clarify what Jesus meant: I am not the flesh-and-blood person you take me for.

Seeing and Believing

Jesus said to him, "Have you believed because you have seen me? Blessed are those who have not seen and yet have come to believe."

(John 20:29)

This passage speaks volumes about the time in which we live, when fundamentalism and biblical research have joined forces to find evidence of Jesus's existence. They search for tombs, written records, and archaeological fragments, in direct contradiction to Jesus's own words. He tells us not to be disappointed that we never met the flesh-and-blood man; it is far better to find Jesus within, through our private search.

God Is Everything

"Whoever believes that the All is itself lacking in anything is himself lacking in everything."

(Thomas 152)

....

The Gnostics took Jesus's antimaterialism and carried it to an even greater extreme. In one pithy sentence, the writer of the Gospel of Thomas says that if you haven't caught on to the fact that God contains everything that exists, you have learned nothing. Verse 148 is just as explicit: "Whoever has come to learn about the world has found only a corpse."

Unity

Jesus gave us the deepest insights into God-consciousness when he talked about himself. Even after two thousand years, we can feel the awe and disbelief that greeted him. The Son of God was robed in the flesh of an ordinary person, and only those who were attuned to higher things could see his real essence. For everyone else, he was either a fraud or a danger—especially to the rich and powerful. It's not as if the case is settled. Skeptics continue to question Jesus's claim to be the Messiah, and faithful Christians harbor doubts about whether Jesus redeemed the world from sin, as he said he did.

Positive or negative images both fail to capture Jesus's essence—complete unity with God. In essence, he is a mystery. And that's the point, to convey to his listeners that being human *is* mysterious. If we list the most important things this mystical figure said about himself, we get a far different picture from the Messiah who will conquer sin and the Romans at the same time.

The mystical Jesus was describing his essence and our own at the same time. This essence is a speck of God, the soul substance inside everyone that never became separated from its source:

Essence is detached from the material world and its concerns.
It turns to God for all its needs.
It acts spontaneously, without a fixed plan.
It sees itself as timeless.
It feels compassion for suffering and wants to end it.
It feels that suffering begins in consciousness and that higher
    consciousness puts an end to suffering.

In describing himself, Jesus was describing the essence that is your source and mine, and we should listen to his words as coming from that place—it is our own inner voice. Jesus set us the challenge of living from our essence, as he did.

I Am Spirit

He said to them, "You are from below, I am from above; you are of this world, I am not of this world."

(John 8:23)

Jesus affirms that he is essentially a spiritual being and that this places him above ordinary understanding. The implication is that higher consciousness cannot easily relate to lower; there is a gap between them that needs to be filled.

I Am Eternal

Jesus said to them, "Very truly, I tell you, before Abraham was, I am."

(John 8:58)

Since Judaism derived from Abraham, Jesus is saying not only that he existed before his physical appearance, but that he came before the founder. This implies that his truth surpasses the eldest of elders. The broader meaning is that spirit surpasses any organized religion.

My Purpose Is to Fulfill

"Do not think that I have come to abolish the law or the prophets; I have come not to abolish but to fulfill."

(Matthew 5:17)

Here Jesus reassures people that he isn't out to overturn their way of life, but of course he is, which is why on other occasions he challenged Jewish belief to its core and called the entire priest caste frauds.

I Bring Freedom

"The Spirit of the Lord is upon me, because he has anointed me to bring good news to the poor. He has sent me to proclaim release to the captives and recovery of sight to the blind, to let the oppressed go free, to proclaim the year of the Lord's favor."

(Luke 4:18–19)

This is an eloquent statement of the Messiah's role as prophesied in the Old Testament. This is also a vivid description of life in spirit, which frees us from our blind perceptions of who we really are.

Work in the Light

"As long as I am in the world, I am the light of the world."

(John 9:5)

This amplifies one of Jesus's most famous sayings. He tells his disciples to concentrate on his works for as long as he will be with them, in effect, to make hay while the sun shines.

I Will Be With You in Spirit

"For where two or three are gathered in my name, I am there among them."

(Matthew 18:20)

The spirit of Jesus is summoned when people gather in his name, but Jesus was also offering a test of truth. His disciples wanted to know how to settle disputes and accusations made against them, and Jesus advised them to go to their accusers in twos and threes to try to convince them of the truth. He caps that advice with this famous statement, making it mystical.

I Am Elusive

"Many times have you desired to hear the words that I say, and there's no one else you could hear them from. There will be days when you will try and seek me but will not find me."

(*Thomas* 73)

The four gospels reiterate that Jesus has come to save the world and will always be present. It takes the Gnostics to be realistic and point out that he can also be very elusive, much like the soul.

My Meaning Is Hidden

"I will give you what no eye has seen and what no ear has heard, what no hand has touched, and what has never been conceived by the mind of man."

(*Thomas* 69)

The Gnostic tendency was always toward extreme, often cryptic mysticism. Are they simply carried away by the spirit of contradiction? Perhaps they were actually being realistic. Jesus existed for them in a state of consciousness beyond the five senses and the thinking mind. This passage is a statement about God-consciousness, not an attempt to mystify for its own sake.

All Authority Is Mine

And Jesus came and said to them, "All authority in heaven and on earth has been given to me."

(Matthew 28:18)

Jesus says these words after he has risen from the dead, appearing to his disciples on a mountain in Galilee. The context is one of revelation. He had promised to attain God's power after he died, and now he has, at a time when Jesus was spirit and no longer a flesh-and-blood person. The deeper teaching is that spirit has authority in the material world as well as in its own domain.

I Serve You

"For who is greater, the one who is at the table or the one who serves? Is it not the one at the table? But I am among you as one who serves."

(Luke 22:27)

This passage takes place as the disciples argue among themselves about who will lead them after Jesus is gone. He tells them, as he does so often, that the leader must be the servant of the others. Speaking here as the voice of spirit, he reminds us that the soul exists to serve.

The World's Savior

"For God so loved the world that he gave his only Son, so that everyone who believes in him may not perish but may have eternal life.

"Indeed, God did not send the Son into the world to condemn the world, but in order that the world might be saved through him."

(John 3:16–17)

Jesus talks about himself more in the Gospel of John than anywhere else. One gets the feeling that the writer of this gospel wanted to confirm who Jesus really was, beyond dispute. The resurrection was fading into memory, and the Romans had destroyed the temple in Jerusalem. In this famous passage, Jesus bolsters his divine identity in the strongest, most eloquent terms. Higher consciousness saves a person from the illusion of death, and this gift comes to us from a loving God.

I Am the Way

Jesus said to him, "I am the way, and the truth, and the life. No one comes to the Father except through me. If you know me, you will know my Father also. From now on you do know him and have seen him."

(John 14:6–7)

When we sift out the element of Church doctrine, Jesus is saying, "If you have been seeking, seek no further. This is how spirit looks when it has been realized." In other words, he brings God-consciousness down-to-earth by being its living exemplar.

I Do God's Will

Then Jesus cried out as he was teaching in the temple, "You know me, and you know where I am from. I have not come on my own. But the one who sent me is true, and you do not know him. I know him, because I am from him, and he sent me."

(John 7:28–29)

Jesus acts not alone, but as a vehicle of God's will. He isn't a person in the way that we think of ourselves as persons. He had no individuality. His will and his purpose belong to God. In the Lord's Prayer he says, "Thy will be done, on earth as it is in heaven," to underline his own experience. In God-consciousness, the small ego merges into the cosmic ego.

I Am God in Action

Jesus said to them, "Very truly, I tell you, the Son can do nothing on his own, but only what he sees the Father doing; for whatever the Father does, the Son does likewise. The Father loves the Son and shows him all that he himself is doing; and he will show him greater works than these, so that you will be astonished. Indeed, just as the Father raises the dead and gives them life, so also the Son gives life to whomsoever he wishes."

(John 5:19–21)

This is a teaching about surrender. At a certain level of consciousness, one's entire self is given to God. Actions no longer come from the ego; they have a divine source. In God-consciousness, a person continues to think and act, but there is no longer the sense that "I" am acting. Instead, God causes things to happen through me. The theme is reinforced again by the gospel: "I have come down from heaven, not to do my own will, but the will of him who sent me." (John 6:38)

Follow My Humility

"You call me Teacher and Lord—and you are right, for that is what I am. So if I, your Lord and Teacher, have washed your feet, you also ought to wash one another's feet. For I have set you an example, that you also should do as I have done to you."

(John 13:13–15)

Jesus spoke of humility many times and in different ways. Here he offers himself as an example. The implication is that spirit exists to serve, and since we are all spirit, our life should be dedicated to service. The ego sees this teaching as a threat, since it wants to become self-important. The truth is that nothing exists except spirit interacting with itself. Therefore, when you serve others, you are servant and master to yourself.

"Tell Me Who I Am"

Jesus said to his disciples, "Find a comparison with someone and tell me what I am like." Simon Peter replied,

"You are like an angel in righteousness." Matthew replied, "You are like a philosopher in wisdom." Thomas replied, "Master, I can't find the words to say whom you are like."

Then Jesus said, "I am not our master. You've been made drunk by drinking from the bubbling spring that flows from me."

(*Thomas* 67)

Just as the writer of John goes to great lengths to underline Jesus's authority, the Gnostics went in the opposite direction. This passage reflects their doctrine of skepticism toward any authority. It's a bit ironic that Jesus is using his own authority to deny it. But that was the Gnostic riddle, how to follow a teacher who didn't want his disciples to follow anyone.

WHO IS THE "REAL" JESUS?

❖

The search for "the real Jesus" is as obsessive today as it has ever been. Throughout the Middle Ages pilgrims made arduous journeys to view a piece of the true Cross or the spear that pierced Jesus's side in the Crucifixion. Cathedrals were built around these purported relics. The jaw of John the Baptist existed in several places, each claiming to possess the genuine article. Fewer relics attract crowds today—the Shroud of Turin is one of the most famous—but the urge to see a physical object associated with Christ remains powerful.

Not long ago, James Cameron, the director of *Titanic,* claimed to have found something even more spectacular than a sunken luxury liner: the final resting place of Jesus and his family. Although the evidence presented wasn't satisfying to the vast majority of biblical scholars, the mass media swarmed over the stone repository for bones inscribed with the names Mary and Joseph. Within weeks came news of another discovery: the tomb of King Herod. Again, the excitement was driven by a longing to find evidence of the real Jesus.

Yet our motives aren't necessarily the same as they were in the

Middle Ages. To a medieval pilgrim, Jesus was undeniably real, and the sacred relics in a cathedral supplied a sense of holy presence; to be near them was to be near God. Modern people, on the other hand, are more legalistic. Our skepticism demands proof that a wandering rabbi actually preached in northern Galilee two thousand years ago. In the absence of such proof, we need to confront the myth of the real Jesus head-on, not for the purpose of bursting a cherished fantasy, but to ensure that the Jesus we choose is closest to the Jesus that can fulfill his teachings. A Jesus who teaches us how to reach God-consciousness lays claim to being more authentic than any other, for even the most basic facts to support the existence of Jesus as he was traditionally worshipped are nonexistent.

Facing this truth is difficult, for the search for the real Jesus has turned into an industry dedicated to feeding the hopes of the faithful. Obviously, this is a thorny issue. Opinions about it run the gamut.

1. *The literal argument:* The real Jesus is in the gospels. There is no need to look any further.
2. *The rationalist argument:* The facts about Jesus have vanished over time. The four gospels are unreliable as evidence about the actual person.
3. *The mystical argument:* The real Jesus was never physical—he is the Holy Spirit.
4. *The skeptical argument:* There was no real Jesus to begin with— he is a figment of theological imagination.
5. *The consciousness argument:* Jesus exists in our own awareness at the level of God-consciousness.

I am a firm believer in the last argument. I believe that Jesus was not only real, but perhaps the most significant person in Western history. Yet in the face of how confusing and contradictory he appears in the four gospels, we must delve deeper, creating a version that fulfills the essence of his teaching.

No doubt countless Christians will be dismayed, even outraged, by a challenge to their image of the real Jesus. So let's examine the arguments in turn. There are pros and cons to each position.

1. *The literal argument:* The real Jesus is in the four gospels. There is no need to look any further.

Pro—This would seem to be the simplest and most logical position for a devout Christian to take. Church tradition has been strong in support of scripture as actual fact. The accounts of Matthew, Mark, and Luke overlap extensively—the Gospel of John is a separate case—corroborating one another on almost everything Jesus said and did. Besides, if the gospels don't offer the real Jesus as he existed in flesh and blood, what other documents could claim more authenticity? Scripture is the best proof we are likely to have.

Con—There is no contrary position if you believe, as fundamentalists do, that the four gospels are divinely revealed. The Church spent most of the last two thousand years without needing to argue any facts at all. But gradually the very notion of what we deem real has shifted. Science undermined blind faith long ago. Now we live in an age when doubt is the starting point. Skeptics put pressure on biblical scholars to offer concrete research, and in that light the four gospels have faltered. They do not meet the test of proven fact.

Emotionally, however, the case is far different. Everyone is aware that a sense of literalism has taken over Christianity. A quick flick of the dial on Sunday morning offers a dozen televangelists touting scripture as beyond doubt, with fire and brimstone as the reward for uncertainty. We need to take special care, therefore, in showing why literalism rests on shaky ground. Fortunately, there is much to bolster the courage of liberal Christians who don't want to be bullied any longer.

Here, then, are some particulars.

The gospels were set down by unknown scribes. Only tradition names Matthew, Mark, Luke, and John as the authors. There is no irrefutable historical evidence that these four figures wrote anything down, and we do not know the nature of their relationship to Jesus when he was alive. This, too, is a matter of tradition.

It is likely that many unknown scribes altered the original texts of the New Testament before a final version was settled on between the third and fourth centuries AD. There is no agreed method for sorting out when a verse entered the gospels or what the original wording might have been.

Whoever may have written these accounts, they do not agree on one time line of events. We don't know, for example, if Jesus taught for three years, as tradition holds, or as little as eighteen months. We don't know if he went to Jerusalem frequently for high holy days or only once on the Passover when he was arrested and crucified.

Words are attributed to Jesus that no one could possibly have heard. (One such instance is the scene in the garden of Gethsemane when Jesus asks God to take away the cup from his lips, meaning his coming doom on the cross. This is also when the text tells us that the disciples had all fallen asleep, without anyone to overhear Jesus's words. Since he was immediately arrested, he would not have had time to recount them, either.) The four gospels also contain too many gaps. There is nothing close to a full biography here. As we saw earlier, except for a single incident in Jerusalem when he was twelve, the gospels offer nothing about Jesus's life between his birth and the immediate time following and his sudden appearance beside the river Jordan to be baptized by John the Baptist when Jesus was around thirty.

The Jesus of the gospels is psychologically incomplete as well. For example, not once does he either smile or laugh. We have to wait for later accounts to learn even the barest facts about his brothers and sisters. Jesus himself rarely refers to any historical or biographical facts. He doesn't speak of his birth in Bethlehem or the miraculous events surrounding it. He doesn't tell us if he is married or single. The twelve disciples were all married, and most of the time their wives accompanied them. Yet no one, least of all Jesus himself, remarks on whether he was married. (Such gaps are so tantalizing that they open Christianity to inventing new myths, such as the one that Jesus married Mary Magdalene. In the wake of the worldwide popularity of *The Da Vinci Code,* it seems that many Christians have no problem dropping the absolute authenticity of the New Testament when it suits them.)

The writers of the gospels set out not to tell the facts of a life but to convert nonbelievers and support their own belief in Jesus as the Messiah. To this end they almost certainly exaggerated events, invented miracles, and put words into Jesus's mouth. (For example, Jesus often directly quotes Old Testament prophecies about the coming Messiah or refers to them. Is this how the actual Messiah spoke or how a messiah has to speak if converts are to be won over?)

Other documents may be as old as the four gospels and therefore make their own claim to authenticity. As we've discussed, these include the so-called Gnostic Gospels, such as the Gospel of Thomas, which are early documents banned by the Church after 313 AD. This was the time when Emperor Constantine officially adopted Christianity, ending the persecution of the faith but beginning a massive effort to destroy heresy and authorize one church and one scripture. Among early Christian congregations, scriptures differed widely. For example, local beliefs had a lot to do with the birth story of Jesus set down in the gospels. The fact that a scribe from a certain church was drawing from local stories probably played a big part.

Mark appears to be the first gospel written, and scholars generally agree that it was based on a lost document (known as Q, from *Quelle,* the German word for "source") thought to have been a list of

Jesus's most important sayings, parables, and teachings. To this bare list Mark added all the stories he could find, which were handed down orally. At a certain point Q disappeared as the popularity of such lists of wise sayings waned.

These facts are daunting. Their cumulative effect is powerful—one might deny any single one, yet taken together they strongly resist denial. Unless you believe that the gospels are revealed truth, there are enough internal problems with the four gospels, I think, to question—and open to interpretation—the Jesus we meet in the Bible.

2. The rationalist argument. The facts about Jesus have vanished over time. The four gospels are unreliable as evidence about the actual person.

Pro—I'm calling this the rationalist position because it bows to a reasonable assumption that most of us would agree with: After the passage of centuries, the real Jesus has been lost. In the early Church, the Gnostic sects went so far as to declare that the four gospels were false. A few of the surviving Gnostic texts (such as the Gospel of Truth) ridicule anyone foolish enough to believe the lies and myths offered up in the accepted account of Jesus.

More generously, modern biblical scholars point out that early gospel writers didn't intend to deceive us, they just wanted to convey the urgency of being converted. If it was necessary to merge fact and fiction, the end justified the means. Hadn't Jesus promised that the Second Coming was very near? Conversion had to happen now in order to avoid eternal damnation. Therefore, liberties were taken, and in the process, all resemblance to a flesh-and-blood person was lost. Only the idealized Jesus survived this process.

Con—Any argument based on the lack of facts about Jesus can be countered by saying that the four gospels are true as a document of belief. Bringing rationality into the argument is a wolf in sheep's clothing. What proof do we have that most of what we call history is authentic? The existence of Julius Caesar isn't supported by photographs, fingerprints, or remains. Devout Christians can argue that Jesus's followers knew him intimately and laid down the facts—meager though they were. The best evidence for this is the new religion that sprang up like wildfire around Christ. Those who witnessed his life story spread the word about what they had actually seen, to great effect.

Both sides of the rationalist argument agree to reject divine revelation. They expect Jesus to be reasonable, differing only in how much doubt is healthy. Only in the past century was it considered permissible to apply the standards of historical biography to Christ. Today he is no longer exempt from the cold eye of the investigator, any more than Shakespeare or Lincoln. Yet research involves comparing one source with another. How can the Bible meet its test when no other documents even show that Jesus existed?

Christians are left in a shadow region full of ambiguities. They must accept the gospels because there is no Jesus without them, while on the other hand, there is no rational way to sort out which part of the story is factual. Physics knows everything about water except how to walk on it. In the end, rationality falls short of providing satisfying answers.

3. The mystical argument: The real Jesus was never physical—he is the Holy Spirit.

Pro—The Gospel of John is famous among biblical scholars for transforming a flesh-and-blood Jesus into a disembodied spirit. The good shepherd gathering his flock shifted to "In the beginning was the Word, and the Word was with God, and the Word was God." (John 1:1) Jesus becomes something abstract and invisible, the Word that was never born and will never die.

John may have pulled Jesus out of history because he had an ulterior motive. Jesus couldn't be the Messiah if he didn't rescue the people of Israel and overturn their oppressors, yet the opposite happened. The Romans destroyed the Second Temple in Jerusalem in 70 AD and with it any hope that Christ would physically rule the world in God's name. There will always be controversy over John's decision to overlay the Jesus story with so much theology, but one thing is certain: He removed the problem of history by making it irrelevant. Jesus belongs to eternity instead.

With the resurrection a flesh-and-blood man was transformed into completely divine substance—the Holy Spirit. There is no need, then, to use history to find the real Jesus. Spirituality is about truths that cannot be understood from a strictly rational perspective. Because the Holy Spirit is transcendent, Jesus must be found not on earth, but in the Kingdom of God. He is a fact of the soul, not of archaeology.

Con—Making Jesus the Holy Spirit begs the question of who is walking through the pages of scripture. Theology is arbitrary; it can tell any story it wants, find any hidden meaning. Once you take a completely mystical view of Jesus, you are exempt from proof. Faith can be neither proved nor disproved. One saint's vision is as good as another's.

The mystical argument offers no compromise with scholars who try to unearth evidence of the real Jesus, leaving humankind facing a terrible rift. On one side lies Jesus's miraculous world, where the physical laws of nature obey his will. On the other side lies the material world, where God doesn't intrude and the physical laws of nature dominate. Where does mysticism begin and leave off? This question can't be answered by mysticism alone. In the past, believers were much more comfortable with a divided reality. Today we want clarity. Is Jesus part of a miraculous world or of this one?

4. The skeptical argument: There was no real Jesus to begin with—he is a figment of theological imagination.

Pro—Those who call the gospels fiction point out that the New Testament is hardly unique. It belongs among many documents in spiritual history that blend hopes, wishes, blind faith, traditional stories, magic, and deeply embedded myths that pervade every culture. From this amalgam, a band of mystical Jews created the very thing they longed for, a messiah who would save Judaism and validate the destiny of the chosen people.

Yet is it credible that a group of people could invent Jesus without a single shred of physical proof? Let's suppose they did. Could they then go on to believe in their own fiction? It's one thing for Dickens to create a character as vivid as Scrooge, but quite another for Dickens to leave money to Scrooge in his will.

An interviewer once asked Albert Einstein if he had been influenced by Christianity, to which Einstein replied, "I am a Jew, but I am enthralled by the luminous figure of the Nazarene." Clearly surprised, the interviewer asked if Einstein believed that Jesus had actually existed. The great scientist replied, "Unquestionably. No one can read the Gospels without feeling the actual presence of Jesus. His personality pulsates in every word. No myth is filled with such life."

Con—The obvious objection to skepticism is that it doesn't solve the mystery of the real Jesus, it only restates it. We already know that faith and reason are at odds. We already know that the gospel writers had their own agenda. To arbitrarily dismiss Jesus as a fiction has no more validity than to arbitrarily accept the whole story as literally true. On the simplest level, it's easier to accept that Jesus existed than that he didn't, because the notion of a new religion spreading like wildfire around a fairy tale is so highly improbable.

What gives pause is the more diluted form of this argument: Jesus was real, but we don't know how real. One could say this was akin to the Gnostic position. The Gnostics believed in Jesus but not the gospel version. Diluted skepticism is similar but reversed. It straddles the fence without coming down for faith alone or reason alone. As such, it doesn't satisfy—emotionally or intellectually. Far better to find a way to have some kind of Jesus (ethical teacher, Messiah, miracle worker, saint, or model of human goodness) than a figure forever relegated to languish in limbo.

5. *The consciousness argument:* Jesus exists in our own awareness at the level of God-consciousness.

Pro—The circumstantial evidence for Jesus's existence is powerful, and since we have no other concrete evidence, accepting it is the best we can do. If Jesus is an invention, those who invented him were spiritually profound. They were touched by the highest level of enlightenment, and it's more likely that this came from one real, living person—a great master—than a group of gospel writers who suddenly became enlightened at the same time.

The life of Buddha gives us a reasonable model to follow: A great teacher transmitted his wisdom to a group of followers, and after his death they tried to preserve his message. Their efforts weren't perfect, but they were impressive. Some disciples became enlightened as a result of following the teaching. Others remained devout believers. All were struck by the wonder of encountering a person whose charisma and wisdom seemed to be superhuman. This was how they transmitted their experience to posterity, leaving records of a flesh-and-blood man whose union with God was immediate, personal, and direct.

Con—I accept the consciousness argument in regard to the real Jesus; therefore, its drawbacks are hard for me to find. A devout Christian would object, certainly, to lumping the Messiah in with enlightened teachers like Buddha and the Vedic sages of India. (Catholicism stoutly resists a Buddha-like Christ, for example, as being inconsistent with Church doctrine. Enlightenment does not trump a belief that all faiths outside Christianity are pagan.)

The uniqueness of Christ has been part of orthodox Christianity for centuries. However, granting Jesus a high level of enlightenment doesn't necessarily demote him; it only makes him more accessible. It places him in the great tradition of wisdom pervading every major culture. The alternative is to wander in the wilderness of theological dispute and wrangle over dubious finds from archaeological sites.

The search for the real Jesus will continue for as long as anyone can foresee. Skepticism will likely continue to rise and faith to decline, as they have for several generations. But whether Jesus remains credible is not the issue. Trying to find "the real Jesus" is basically a fundamentalist effort. As such, it plays into the agenda of people who want Christianity to be rigid and exclusionary. The tragic irony is that Jesus preached against the priests in the temple for taking just that position.

All the arguments I've outlined here rest on interpretation. Despite the strictures of the Church, which hold that only priests and saints have authority in this area, today there is a level playing field in religion: Anyone can devise a new interpretation of the New Testament. Unfortunately, this great text is ambiguous and confusing enough to support almost any thesis about its meaning.

The salvation Jesus offered was the same as Buddha's: release from suffering and a path to spiritual freedom, joy, and closeness to God. In that light, the real Jesus is as available today as he ever was, perhaps more so. Instead of relying on faith alone, we can go beyond worship to find a body of teachings consistent with the world's wisdom traditions, a corroboration in Christian terms that higher consciousness is real and open to all.

Part Three

TAKING JESUS AS
YOUR TEACHER

A GUIDE FOR SEEKERS

THE SEARCH FOR
HIGHER REALITY

Jesus opened a path to enlightenment that is still viable today. From his teachings we learn how to create a shift in our own awareness. To support this process, I am going to provide daily exercises based on verses from the New Testament. Jesus did not supply specific practices beyond prayer and giving oneself to God through faith. Yet two thousand years later we know a great deal about spiritual growth from both Eastern and Western traditions.

Jesus asks us for personal transformation. But Jesus isn't reachable as a personality. He exists in awareness as the state of unity with God. Every step that brings you out of separation and closer to unity is valuable. We are each bound up in limited perception about who we are; the purpose of the following exercises is to replace outworn assumptions, breaking down obstacles that make it seem right and proper to exist in limitation.

God-consciousness is something you can work toward today. The Church has postponed redemption until some far-off Judgment Day. Fortunately, God is everywhere. Feeling that you are disconnected from God means that you have made a mistake. The purpose of the spiritual path is to correct that mistake. This implies a change in the way we live and also in how we see ourselves. In this chapter I will outline how such changes occur on a practical basis. The fifteen steps given here aren't Church doctrine, and at first glance my application of Jesus's words may feel unfamiliar. But Jesus cannot be seen in isolation. He belongs to a world tradition. His teachings merge seamlessly with the stream of wisdom flowing from other traditions as well as from Christianity in its later evolution.

Fifteen Steps to God-Consciousness: Lessons and Exercises

1. The Kingdom of Heaven is within you.

Applying the teaching—The source of reality is inside you. It is your essence.

Here Jesus points the way to hidden dimensions, not simply the conventional notion of Heaven. When you go inside, you are aware of activity such as thoughts and feelings. Your instinct is to pursue the activity that brings pleasure and avoid that which brings pain. But Jesus speaks of a completely different inner reality. The consciousness hidden behind your thoughts is the consciousness that upholds all intelligence in the universe. It is personal and collective at the same time. The personal is made up of your relationships, the collective is made up of the myths and archetypes common to all cultures. Both dimensions are you, and you can begin to connect the two as a bridge to the sacred.

Exercise—Sit quietly when you have time to be alone and undisturbed. Choose a prayer that you feel comfortable with—or better yet, a meaningful phrase from that prayer. Usually I ask people to say, "Our Father, who art in Heaven," but you may prefer "Hail

Mary, full of grace." Silently repeat the words to yourself, letting them settle naturally into your awareness, becoming softer and deeper. Continue for at least five minutes and up to twenty minutes. This kind of sacred repetition is common to every religious tradition.

When you open your eyes, let your gaze settle on a sacred image, such as an icon, a picture of Jesus, a statue of Mary. Ask this figure to embody itself through you. Gently feel a connection. Don't force this, just put out the intention that the archetype of Christ, Mary, or a chosen saint merges with your being. Some people use angels for this purpose, which is the same as asking for the essence of God to reach you.

Now contemplate the specific qualities you want, such as love, compassion, or forgiveness. These are archetypal energies that you are asking to express through your thoughts, emotions, and actions. By calling on your higher archetype, you will find yourself thinking and doing things you never expected as the person you know. Although Jesus refers to God as the Father, spirit isn't bound by gender. Like the Gnostics, you may conceive of God as feminine or inclusive of both genders.

This exercise works to remove the artificial boundary between the isolated ego-self and the higher self.

2. Be in the world but not of it.

Applying the teaching—Through detachment, you master both inner and outer reality.

Jesus is asking for detachment, which isn't the same thing as indifference or passivity. This is an important distinction. You are more than the flesh-and-blood person you see in the mirror, a person created by the world around you. Your actual being has its source in spirit. Through detachment you shift your allegiance away from the physical toward the spiritual. Since you are spirit first and an individual person second, the world is actually in you, as images, thoughts, sensations, memories, and projections. You are more real than the material world and closer to the creative source.

Exercise—You can sit for this exercise at first, but it is meant to be used at any time, even in activity. Center yourself for a moment, then become aware of your breath going in and out. Be mindful of its flow, how the breath is constantly changing in subtle or obvious ways. At the same time, be mindful of the background of your breathing. This is the ground of being and silence, the ground of yourself. Notice how both aspects coexist, the changing and the nonchanging. You can be in the world of change while remembering the ground of nonchange.

Breath and spirit have always been connected; there is a subtle link between inspiration and respiration. If you are mindful of this link, it will strengthen. Being mindful of your breathing is in fact one of the most natural ways to find detachment from the turmoil around you.

3. *For my yoke is easy and my burden is light.*

Applying the teaching—Life becomes more effortless as you move closer to God-consciousness.

Jesus speaks on two levels here, one higher and one lower. The lower level, the physical, is full of burdens, but Jesus assures his followers that God will open the way and remove obstacles, sometimes through miraculous means. This is the same as saying that life on the spiritual path is much easier than the struggle of everyday life.

On a higher level, Jesus is using the voice of pure spirit. The soul is saying, "Be at one with me. If you do, your struggles will end." In the East this is the promise of yoga, or union with God. The Sanskrit word *yoga* is also the root for the English word *yoke*. It's not a stretch to hear Jesus saying, "Union with me is easy, my burden is light." This is an inspiring reminder whenever you are tempted to think of Jesus as a tragic figure fated to shoulder the burdens of a sinful world.

Exercise—In whatever way you can today, go with the flow. Do not resist or oppose. Do not control. Proceed through your day without expectations. The world seems to be a huge entity and you a very small one. But in truth the world is flowing from you. You are its source. To realize that truth, you must start to live as if it is true.

You can think of this as an input-output exercise. When you operate out of a belief that the real world "out there" is pushing against you, your mental input manifests as obstacles, resistance, and struggle. But if you operate from the belief that you are the source and the world is secondary, then events will move smoothly, with time and room to spare. Solutions to problems will begin to come effortlessly.

In practical terms, the best advice is to hang loose. When you meet a familiar situation that angers or frustrates you, don't fall back on your old reactions. You won't benefit by doing more of what didn't work in the first place. Allow God, spirit, the soul, to take over, even in a small degree. Wait and see what the universe has in mind. You will be surprised at how powerful this exercise can be once you dedicate yourself to it.

The universe cooperates with you once you know that your desire and God's desire are the same.

4. Ask, and you will receive.

Applying the teaching—All fulfillment comes from within.

This may seem to be one of Jesus's most extravagant promises. We have all asked and not received. To find out what Jesus actually meant, then, we have to answer a few questions: Who is asking? Where is the request going? Whom does it reach? For most people, the asking comes from the ego, with its unending stream of desires.

The request is going out into empty space or to a vaguely remem-bered God from childhood. The receiver of the request is unknown.

What this means is that asking and receiving are disconnected. Indeed, they must be, because in everyday awareness the world is separate from us and fragmented into millions of isolated events. However, at a deeper level everything is unified and whole. When you ask for anything, the One is asking the One, God is asking God. And there is always a response.

Exercise—Learn to ask in a new way, by expecting every wish to bring a response. Take the attitude expressed by the Persian poet Rumi: "Ask all of yourself." The mechanics of giving and receiving are inside you. Therefore, the next time you pray for something, or simply desire it, go through the following steps:

Express the desired outcome to yourself clearly.
Detach yourself from your request after you make it.
Take an undemanding attitude to the outcome.
Be open to whatever response the universe gives back.
Know that there is always a response.

In this case, "response" doesn't mean a yes or no from God. There is no judge deciding whether you are worthy or not. Those perceptions were born of separation. When Jesus told his followers that God sees and knows everything, he was describing the com-plete intimacy between the self and the intelligence that pervades the universe. Since you could not exist without being part of that intelligence, praying to God is circular, a feedback loop.

The purpose of taking a new attitude toward prayer isn't so that you can get more than you have in the past. As with every aspect of the spiritual path, the purpose is to overcome separation. In the state of unity that Jesus experienced, every thought brought a response from God. In the state of separation that his followers experienced, many thoughts seemed to get no response. This represented a breakdown of communication. To restore it required a new sense of self. Jesus repeatedly teaches that "you are in God, and God is in you." Gradually, we can begin to experience this truth, and one of the best ways is by observing how our prayers are answered. The ways are often subtle, and they change. For example, if you pray to be healed from sickness, any and all of the following are possible:

You recover completely and spontaneously.

Current medical treatment is effective.

Your condition shows signs of improving faster than normal or with fewer side effects and lingering trauma.

You become more confident that you will recover.

Your fear and anxiety over being sick begin to lessen.

A sense of peace comes to you.

You gain acceptance.

By being open and alert to these responses, some of which are inner and others outer, you escape the dichotomy of "God healed me" and "God didn't heal me." Every prayer is one tiny part of an eternal journey. The ego-mind dwells in duality, and it's used to expecting yes or no answers. In reality, the journey has countless nuances; every single event is interconnected with every other. Therefore, when you ask for anything, the response to your wish is computed in the context of every aspect of your self, past, present, and future.

The richness of prayer is twofold, then. It opens you up to a universe that lives and breathes, a universe that can actually respond to the slightest thought. More important, prayer shows you that an intimate connection with God not only is possible, but is the most natural way to live. All fulfillment is from within, because every event begins and ends at the level of the soul.

5. *Forgive us our trespasses, as we forgive those who trespass against us.*

Applying the teaching—Suffering is rooted in unreality. You can go beyond suffering by seeking what is real.

In this passage from the Lord's Prayer, Jesus touches on one of his main goals, to make people believe in a forgiving God. In standard Christian belief, Jesus forgave the sins of the world and brought about a new covenant with God based on the forgiveness of sin rather than divine punishment. You need to ask yourself if this is what you experience. Do you feel that your past wrongdoing has been erased from your conscience? Have you forgiven others who wronged you in the past?

The teaching here is really about how to end suffering. Sin is the cause of suffering in the Christian model. You cannot be forgiven your sins, and thus released from suffering, unless you are aware that you have been forgiven. The message of forgiveness has to reach you, and that requires the removal of whatever blocks it: guilt, anger, resentment, lack of self-worth, and isolation. If these obstacles can be removed, you will experience divine forgiveness as Jesus promised it. You don't have to adopt a religious framework; forgiveness can be interpreted as coming from the soul, the unconscious, or spirit—whatever place you accept as your source.

Exercise—Guilt is a form of suffering, and the root of suffering is unreality. Jesus constantly emphasized that his listeners did not know who he was or where he came from. They were trapped in an unreal vision of God and human beings alike. To forgive yourself or anyone else, you must move in the direction of reality. As described by Jesus, what's real is God's love and forgiveness and the infinite worth of his children here on earth.

You need to reinforce this reality in any way you can. Follow the

Golden Rule and treat others as you would want to be treated. Be grateful for your life. Look for ways to appreciate others. All these things begin a process of purifying hidden feelings of guilt and resentment. Let those feelings come up. You don't want to mask them over. Seeming to forgive when that is what you really feel isn't productive.

If there is something in your past that you feel especially guilty about, sit quietly and go through the following steps:

Visualize what you feel guilty about. See the scene where it occurred. Feel the way it felt.

Spend a few moments releasing your guilty feelings. If this requires you to cry, take deep breaths, or lie down because your feelings are so intense, follow your instincts. But don't indulge your guilt. Tell yourself that these feelings are leaving. Ask for them to be lifted from you.

When you feel that you are directly confronting your guilt, tell yourself that all the images and sensations you are experiencing are nothing but memories. As such, they have no present reality. Don't fight to make them go away, since that doesn't work. Emotional attachments cause memories to linger. But emotions from the past are also unreal; they are shadows casting darkness on the present moment.

Express a willingness to let go of what isn't real. Ask the old feelings and stuck energies to dissipate and return to their source. Listen for a response. Guilt, like any stuck energy, grows louder and stronger in the mind when it isn't heeded. It's like a microchip constantly repeating the same message. Don't mistake this intensity for proof that you are bad and what you did will never be forgiven. The intensity is nothing more than a cry to get your attention. So pay attention, and as you do, express your sympathy and understanding.

Having gotten this far, you are at the point of forgiveness. You have seen that suffering is a residue from the past built up from unreleased energies. Forgiveness is actually release. It isn't an act of moral courage or superhuman tolerance. The best metaphor is purification. Like letting cloudy water settle into clarity, your aim is to remove the haziness that keeps you from seeing who you really are, a soul free from guilt. Don't expect to remove all the murkiness at once. This is a process, and you need to repeat it for as long as necessary. Know that the process works. If you confront the shadows and ghosts of past suffering, present suffering will lift, and a space will be created for lasting forgiveness.

6. *Be still and know that I am God.*

Applying the teaching—Life unfolds spontaneously and effortlessly from the source.

These words come from the Psalms rather than Jesus, who did not leave behind any equivalent teaching. Being still refers to meditation, and although Jesus didn't teach meditation, it became an essential aspect of Christian tradition. Along with prayer, meditation is the principal way that a believer establishes a link with God and Jesus. One might say that meditation was implied when Jesus said, "Abide in me as I abide in you."

I want to shift our focus somewhat and look to the meaning of "be still." If we take meditation to be an isolated activity, something you do when you want to find an oasis of peace and calm, we miss the larger point. The purpose of meditation is to contact reality. There is no special benefit to silence per se. Rather, the mind's incessant activity distracts it from what lies below the level of activity. Silence is only one aspect, and not the most important. At the source, you are connected to pure awareness, the wellspring of all intelligence, power, and organizing ability. If you allow yourself to be still, you can begin to observe these qualities at work, both inside yourself and beyond. "Know that I am God" refers to the unfolding of a deeper reality than the ego-mind was ever aware existed.

Exercise—Whenever you find yourself in a state of uncertainty, sit quietly and go inward. When you feel centered, remind yourself that a larger scheme is at work. Hidden intelligence is organizing every aspect of your life, even though at any given moment you may catch only a glimpse. To resolve your uncertainty, you need to expand beyond the limitation imposed by confusion, fear, control, and rigid expectations.

See yourself in your present contracted state and relax. Visualize yourself expanding; take a deep breath and let your boundaries move outward on the exhale. Contraction is both a physical and a mental state. To be in spirit, and ultimately in union with God, we go beyond boundaries. Because all the walls of separation are self-constructed, the self can bring them down.

It's useful every day to look at the limitations holding you back, but don't expect the walls to fall completely or all at once. You will be engaged in a long negotiation with your old beliefs and self-conception. Everyone has countless reasons for believing in the separate self, for staying away from the truth of their own divine nature. The present exercise forms only a single component of loosening the grip of limitation. By sitting quietly and seeing yourself expanding beyond the ego-personality, you will come to realize new things, until eventually the deepest knowledge dawns and you recognize God's reality.

7. *As you sow, so shall you reap.*

Applying the teaching—The world is a mirror of the self.

These words have already come up in the context of Karma—Jesus is teaching his listeners that their actions have moral consequences. Good actions lead to good results, bad actions to bad results: That is the most common understanding of Karma. But in a broader sense Jesus is making a point about life on the spiritual path. The world is a mirror of the self. The reason that good actions lead to good results isn't that God listens in, makes a judgment, and then rewards you with a good result. Instead, action and result occur simultaneously.

There is a constant, instantaneous calculus taking place with your every thought, word, and action. Most people don't notice good or bad results unless these are dramatic, but the world functions as a mirror down to the minutest detail. The mechanics of consciousness are set up so that inner and outer dimensions match perfectly. Why does it take Jesus or another enlightened master to point this out? Because the mind is so complex and human nature so multilayered that we are easily conditioned to overlook the links between inner and outer. Separation is based on our own willingness to ignore certain images, some of them upsetting and disturbing, that the world reflects back at us. On the spiritual path, you become more willing to see what is right before your eyes—if not the eyes of the body, then the eyes of the soul.

Exercise—This is an exercise to teach you how to look into the mirror. You are going to see yourself in two people, someone you greatly admire and someone you intensely dislike. Begin with the person you admire. Make a list of his or her most admirable traits. Try to be as personal as possible. There are many strong, courageous role models, for example, so why did you choose Nehru in particular, or Mother Teresa, or Martin Luther King Jr.? The answer is that your own aspirations match your hero's achievement. Some quality in you seeks to emerge. It may be the seed of compassion that is drawn upward by Mother Teresa or the seed of altruism drawn upward by Albert Schweitzer. If you pick Jesus, a figure so immense that he belongs to the whole world, look at your own desire to expand in all dimensions; perhaps the seed of freedom wants to grow.

Now reverse the exercise and pick someone you intensely dislike. Write down that person's worst qualities (this part usually isn't very hard) and then consider how you also embody those qualities without being able to see them in yourself. We project onto others what we cannot face in ourselves. Try to avoid picking someone universally hated like Adolf Hitler, because the enormity of his actions may drive you further from seeing yourself. It's better to choose someone closer to your own life.

This exercise becomes truly valuable when you carry out both parts. The world is not just a mirror but a teaching mirror. It exposes you to your present situation in its entirety. When Jesus spoke of abiding in God, he pointed to the highest purpose of the world as mirror: to show you that God infuses all things so completely that nothing can be seen but him, divinity in all directions extending to eternity. You live and abide in that reality, and when you begin to see that the mirror exists, reflections that were once only about your daily existence expand to encompass the soul, which is the real you. Yet even before you catch such soul glimpses, learning to look into the world as a mirror helps to heal separation, as you see that you are included in creation, not living in some private exile outside it.

8. Resist not evil.

Applying the teaching—Evil is the collective and personal shadow.

One effect of divine grace, as Jesus taught it, was to counter evil. Just as judgment is left to the Lord, so is punishing evil. Jesus uses conventional vocabulary at times when he speaks about Satan and possession by demons, but what rings far more true is his teaching that evil should not be resisted. As we saw earlier, learning how to overcome evil without resisting it involves a process. Jesus isn't calling for instant conversion to pacifism, nor is he asking us to be blind to the terrible effects of evil when it goes unchecked.

What he is teaching changes as you pass through the stages of your own spiritual path. Reality is different in different states of consciousness, and that includes evil. You cannot pretend to love your enemy, yet when you come closer to God-consciousness, such compassion comes naturally. It's helpful to remind yourself that evil isn't a monolith or a constant. It has many shades and degrees, and once they are fully examined, evil turns out to be your own shadow self expressing outwardly what you haven't resolved inwardly.

Exercise—Evil, like everything else, depends upon perception. As your perception changes, evil shifts. It's very important that this shift occurs, because if you remain locked in a rigid hatred or fear of evil, you push your own shadow further out of sight. No matter how hard you struggle to overcome evil, unless you understand your own shadow, it will find new ways to bring back the thing you hate and fear.

Brooding on your negative traits isn't going to bring the shadow to light. One act that will is confession. Find someone you feel you can trust. For many people, the only person might be a complete stranger, or it might be an entire support group whose purpose is healing. At a time that feels right to you, divulge something you feel ashamed or guilty about. Don't begin with a serious crime or transgression. The aim here isn't to confess to God, but to relate to your shadow in a new way.

The shadow can be defined as the hidden area of the self where forbidden feelings are hidden. These feelings cover a wide range, including anger, revenge, jealousy, prejudice, rampant sexual desire, and murderous rage. There is so much to uncover that people find it difficult to begin. We all have a stake in being accepted, and the shadow contains all in us that is most unacceptable. Confession in the religious sense couldn't cope with the emptying out of every dark place. The only way to disarm the shadow is to relate to it in a different way, and when you reveal a secret to someone, your life in hiding begins to shift.

Evil is never pure and rarely simple. It is rooted in a collection of factors. Instead of resorting to words like "evil" or "sinful," go into the following areas:

Why am I hiding this bad thought, impulse, or action?

What am I ashamed of?

How do I think I am going to be hurt if this is exposed?

Am I being affected by memories of past punishment?

When I hear an inner voice judging me harshly, who from my past is actually speaking to me?

How would my self-image suffer if I revealed this?

Have I been working within a belief system that sees human beings as innately sinful?

Why do I choose to live with guilt instead of without it?

You need to ask all these questions every time you step into the region of the shadow. The encounters aren't pleasant, but they are strengthening, and they bring the truth to light. The truth is that evil has power over you only if you give it power. It takes a series of mistaken decisions to compile a case against you. When you ask the questions just given, you are retracing your steps so that you can take back those mistaken assumptions and beliefs.

As you begin to reexamine your history in a new light, you can rehabilitate the shadow. It poses as your enemy largely in reaction to your own guilt and fear. The shadow can't be abolished, so don't try. Creation is a construct of light and darkness, and so are you. It's this fact, the eternal play of good and evil, that Jesus wants people to see, in order that they can rise to a higher plane of existence. He doesn't ask us to conquer evil. Struggling against evil only brings more energy into its grasp. But if you stop resisting evil and come to terms with it instead, you will be taking steps toward the ultimate realization that evil is a wound inflicted in separation and healed in unity.

9. *In my father's house are many mansions.*

Applying the teaching—Existence is multidimensional. Therefore, your own life is multidimensional.

These words were offered as reassurance to the disciples when they were afraid of losing Jesus and worried about the future of their souls. He promises to prepare a place for them in Heaven—in modern translations, "mansions" is often replaced with "rooms" or "dwelling-places." I don't think that Jesus meant anything as simple as "There's plenty of room in Heaven." He is referring to God's omnipresence—or, as we might say, the many dimensions that divine consciousness pervades.

People remain anxious about going to Heaven and whether or not a place has really been made for them there. On the spiritual path, however, you discover that you are multidimensional. The belief that your life is confined to the material world derives from a very narrow focus of perception, when in fact you exist simultaneously on every plane. If you liberate yourself from perceived limitations, you can experience the "many mansions" that Jesus refers to without waiting until you go to Heaven. All dimensions are included in one consciousness, and as an aspect of that consciousness, you are allowed the freedom to participate in whatever level you choose.

Every dimension of consciousness has its own reality. To think, imagine, wish, and dream is an activity in consciousness, and although we don't commonly think of dreaming as a voyage into another dimension, it certainly can be described that way. More important, if you see yourself going beyond the physical, often you are doing just that. In other cultures, people use dreams to create the events of the next day. They accept as completely natural that visions can come true.

Exercise—In Jesus's teaching, the communication between different dimensions was completely open—faith performed miracles because being open to God was enough to create a living connection to his limitless power. You can create this connection by going inward and acting on the subtle level by using visualization. Sit with eyes closed and see yourself walking through a familiar place, such as a park or your neighborhood. In your mind's eye, see every detail around you, smell the air, let everything in the environment come to you. Don't force yourself to see, just be open to what is around you.

What surprises people when they perform this exercise is that they often see entirely new and unexpected things. They find a lost object or notice something they never realized was there. This is just a first step. People can visualize events from a great distance or go into rooms they haven't visited before. What they come to realize is that in fact this isn't an exercise in imagination. It's an exercise in merging the material world with the subtle world. They find themselves actually going to another place without having to travel there physically.

You can take the exercise as far as you would like. I have asked people to go on guided tours of Heaven and Hell, as they imagine such places to be. They come back with intense experiences. Human beings participate in creating all the heavens and hells in cultures around the world by envisioning these dimensions and then believing in their own creations. No child is loved as fiercely as a child of the mind. Love, belief, and attachment are powerful creative tools. They solidify perception into reality. The various ancient gods and goddesses were given all-too-human attributes. The difference between the vengeful God of the Old Testament and the loving God of the New Testament is that human consciousness was ready for a shift in perception.

Your inner world is filled with images you have already brought to life. You are the author of many things you fear, and you always have the choice to make those fears vanish. The technique here is a variation on the basic exercise. Sit with eyes closed and see the thing you most fear. Allow yourself to experience your racing heart, tight chest, or shallow breathing—whatever reaction anxiety may produce. When you feel a little calmer, start manipulating the images. Make them grow bigger and smaller. Make them stop. Make time go back and forth. The grip of fear is rigid, and you can loosen it by showing yourself that you have control over your own mental images. Nobody put them in your head but yourself. It's an illusion to believe that they have control over their own creator.

In short, what you are doing here is reclaiming authorship over your own life. Visualization isn't just a means of seeing a good outcome in advance, although that is how many people use it. It's a means of connecting your own power at the subtle level to the external events that constantly well up from your inner world. Ultimately, the faith that performs miracles is faith in your own divine nature.

10. *You must be born from above.*

Applying the teaching—To renew yourself, die to the old every day.

Jesus spoke about death as a prelude to resurrection, and he also spoke about the need to be born again. The connection between the two was summed up by Paul as "dying unto death." Christian doctrine has focused almost entirely on trusting in the resurrection of Jesus as a sign that every soul will be resurrected one day. But when he said, "You must be born from above," Jesus put the emphasis on transformation in this lifetime, not some faraway future.

Being born from above means a rebirth in spirit. For me, the best way to imagine such an event isn't by accepting Jesus as personal lord and savior, although fundamentalists constantly demand that. Spiritual rebirth usually isn't a single event, a blinding epiphany that causes one's life to change from that moment forward.

Some individuals may be able to organize their spiritual life around one dramatic breakthrough, but for most, spiritual rebirth is a process akin to the long process that causes people to mature psychologically. The spiritual process brings transformation steadily, one step at a time, yet the overall result is dramatic. One's attachment to the ego and its belief in separation, including the ultimate separation of death, is being jettisoned.

Exercise—If being born again is a process, you can contribute to it every day. In fact, this is the only viable way to creatively shape the spiritual path so that it belongs to you personally. Right now, you accept a fixed set of labels that define you. These include your name, age, family, occupation, and social status. From Jesus's perspective, however, none of these labels is the true you; they distract from the reality that you are spirit embodied in flesh. If you wanted to, you could redefine yourself every day. As the fixed self gives way to a dynamic, fluid self that is open to the unknown, freedom dawns. In that freedom, you go beyond death by discovering that you encompass life and death in a state of pure Being.

Now let's translate this into practical applications. Write down the most basic labels that apply to you: name, age, gender, education level, and occupation. Taking one at a time, consider how each label defines you. For example: Your name specifies the identity of a person with a certain family background, it locates you in time and space, it isolates you from others, and it becomes part of your self-image. You are attached, to varying degrees, to all these threads of identity. Now consider whether these connections must apply. Do you feel a need to conform to family traditions and expectations? Is it important to you that your name earns recognition? As you ask such basic questions, you can begin to free yourself from the threads of attachment that keep you from being "born from above."

Now you can take steps to redefine yourself. If you spot yourself thinking in a certain way because it is appropriate to your age, education level, gender, or social status, ask yourself if there are other ways to think. If you open yourself, you will be amazed at how thoroughly you have been defined by rigid beliefs and outdated conditioning. These external influences aren't the real you, and until you go through the process of detaching yourself from old definitions, you cannot confront the unknown. Everything new that comes your way winds up passing through a filtering process until it fits your likes and dislikes, social status, income, education level, and so on. Spiritual experience is unfiltered; it comes directly and spontaneously. The best way to prepare yourself to encounter spirit is to learn to be willing to redefine yourself every day.

11. You are the light of the world.

Applying the teaching—The universe thinks and acts through you.

In an earlier chapter, this verse was discussed at length. Here we can expand on its personal implications. One application of Jesus's words is this: The universe thinks and acts through you. You are not the result of physical forces that have driven all of creation, with human intelligence being a late-stage by-product. Rather, a universal intelligence is experiencing itself through countless forms. You are one form of this intelligence, and yet you are also the whole. Just as a cell in the body is expressing the body's wholeness, you are expressing the wholeness of creation at this very minute.

Ordinary perception cannot see the whole, which is why Jesus spoke so much about making the blind to see. He asked his followers to develop what has been called "second attention," or divine sight, the ability to know yourself as pure Being, beyond boundaries. When Jesus promised his followers that they would accomplish the same miracles he had performed and even greater, he was speaking from second attention. Just as he didn't see himself in limitation, neither did he see them that way. To be the light of the world, you must understand that the world itself is light—that is, pure awareness manifesting in physical form.

Exercise—To develop second attention, you must attune yourself to it. First attention focuses on the material world; it dwells on appearance rather than essence. The light that Jesus referred to is invisible to the eye but apparent to the soul. When you think, say, or do anything, you are manipulating consciousness, or to put it another way, you are using the stuff of awareness to create something. Just as jet fuel disappears in order to make a plane fly, consciousness disappears when it is used. Its potential turns into some sensation, thought, object, or event. As you read that last sentence, you were transforming consciousness without being aware that it was flowing through you.

Jesus asks us to see through this disappearing act. Through second attention, you can perceive yourself as awareness itself, not as one of its products and creations. There are many ways to catch such glimpses.

Meditating to reach inner silence.
Sensing the purity of Nature.
Sudden flashes of innocence.
An impulse of love.
An intuitive connection to your muse.
Sensing inner guidance, a source of wisdom.
A feeling that you belong in the larger scheme of life.

Consider if you have ever experienced such things; begin to notice them now, and be on the lookout for those moments when you can sense that something lies behind the veil of appearances. Even though we all live by first attention and therefore lose ourselves in constant activity, we are also equipped to perceive the world through second attention.

Whenever you have a flash of love, innocence, inspiration, awe, wonder, or joy, remind yourself: This is the real me. Don't let such moments simply pass you by. Stop and appreciate them, and ask that you receive more in the future. In this way you open a feedback loop between first and second attention. You will continue to view the physical world as such, but its significance will change. You will start to see consciousness at work, Being in motion. In this way, the realms of change and nonchange begin to merge. Light starts to enter the world, until the world is eventually seen as made of light and nothing else. Jesus experienced his existence that way and promised his followers that one day they would, too.

12. So do not worry about tomorrow.

Applying the teaching—Trust in the organizing power of the universe.

Jesus explicitly told his followers not to earn a living, save money, plan ahead, or worry about the future. The quoted phrase is a fragment of that teaching, but the rest of the Sermon on the Mount reinforces that point again and again. If he was offering one of his most radical injunctions, it became the least followed. Like everyone else, Christians worry, plan, earn a living, and amass money and possessions.

This teaching isn't viable in ordinary consciousness, yet if you apply it on the spiritual path, asking for change beyond the ordinary, something new begins to emerge. A random, mindless universe is transformed into a safe haven, a home for every person, filled with life's necessities. Jesus called this safe haven Providence because its purpose is to provide. Learning to trust Providence is a process. The old ways to which you are used to clinging gradually change. Even though Jesus tells his disciples to divest themselves of their money and possessions, I think we must assume a special relationship there. They had an enlightened teacher to guide them into far more radical change than any of us would be prepared for. Yet we need to be true to the underlying meaning of this teaching: God can be trusted. Your ego does not need to take over the function of Providence; there are other ways to attain life's abundance.

Exercise—If we take Jesus literally, the most direct way not to worry about tomorrow is to live in the present. Only the present is real. It contains the fullness of the world and the fullness of spirit at the same time. But the present is elusive. We all lead our lives by remembering the past and anticipating the future. Therefore, the real and unreal are inexorably blended. They are so entangled, in fact, that the present must be retrieved piecemeal; you cannot leap into it all at once.

If you examine it one quality at a time, the present moment is composed of the following:

Alertness—being awake.

Openness—or being free from expectations.

Freshness—not being overshadowed by the past.

Innocence—not judging from old experience.

Spontaneity—allowing new impulses to come in without criticism or censorship.

Fearlessness—the absence of traumas from the past.

Replenishing—the capacity to renew oneself from within.

All of these qualities are present inside you; young children display them all the time. So your aim isn't to learn how to be spontaneous, innocent, fearless, and the rest, but to uncover them once more. Right now, the present moment is full for you, but in an unreal way. It is full of memories, expectations, projected beliefs, and past conditioning. The present moment could be full in a different, far more real way, through all the qualities just listed.

You must challenge yourself to move from the unreal to the real.

Take any quality on the list and look at how much you rely on its opposite.

> Dull instead of alert.
> Closed off instead of open.
> Stale instead of fresh.
> Knowing instead of innocent.
> Planned or routine instead of spontaneous.
> Anxious instead of fearless.
> Depleting instead of replenishing.

These opposite qualities come from the part of you that thinks it knows about life already. The ego relies on the familiar. It is reluctant to experience the unknown, which is the very essence of life. There is no such thing as knowing how to be spontaneous or knowing how to be innocent. By definition, a spontaneous impulse is unpredictable. You can't take the spiritual journey with a foot in two boats. It's futile to try to find a compromise that includes knowingness and innocence, anxiety and fearlessness, or any other pair of opposites.

The only way to retrieve the present is to clear out the past, which means whatever is routine, dull, knowing, calculated, anxious, and traumatic. You cannot manufacture innocence, for example, but by removing its opposite, knowingness, you leave space so that innocence can express itself once more. When confronted with someone you think you know very well, whose behavior is predictable, don't react at first. Leave a place for something new in your perception of this person. Ask a new kind of question, agree where you would normally disagree, withhold judgment, and see what happens. The same process can be applied to every other quality of the present moment. Distance yourself from past expectations, and in that way something unexpected can emerge.

13. Abide in me as I abide in you.

Applying the teaching—You will be free when you no longer see yourself in isolation.

Jesus often makes statements that are inspiring because only the Messiah could say them. When he says, "The Father and I are one," or "Abide in me as I abide in you," we don't apply those words to ourselves. Yet we should. Consciousness is a shared phenomenon. No one is isolated from it, and when Jesus speaks from the level of spirit, he is speaking for all human beings. On the spiritual path you become less isolated as an individual and more universal as an expression of consciousness. This change occurs because in truth everything is happening in consciousness.

I realize how convincing it is to see yourself as a unique person standing apart from others. How can it be that they exist in you and you in them? Consider a simple example. When I remember my mother's face, it exists in my awareness, conjured up in the mind. But the same thing is true when my mother was alive and I met her in person. The photons of light that hit my retina and registered in my brain as an image of her face created a delay. It took only a few milliseconds for my brain to register that I was seeing my mother, but by the time it did, she was a memory. The image in my brain came after the fact, much like the light from a star. Therefore, even in life she existed as a stream of memories in my awareness. There is nowhere else to find her except in me. What holds true for the sense of sight also holds true for the other senses. If she touched my hand, I registered that, too, through brain activity after the fact.

Jesus went further. He taught that the spiritual aspect of a person also exists in awareness. But unlike the sight of my mother, her spirit comes from a shared source; we are all part of God, the soul, the Holy Spirit. When Jesus said, "I am in you," he was refer-ring to his essence. In the state of separation you aren't aware of essence; the soul level of our existence appears to be far away. But as you progress on the spiritual path, qualities like empathy and compassion start to grow. By entering another person's situation, by sharing and bonding, you begin to have the experience of literally abiding in someone else. God-consciousness carries this transformation to its final end. You are in everyone else, and everyone else is in you. Instead of perceiving any human being as an individual person, you see them as essence, or pure Being.

Exercise—At the quantum level we are all blinking in and out of existence countless times per minute. So everyone and everything you see is in flux. Your brain creates the illusion of constancy, yet in truth the person or thing you believe to be in front of you is actually a ghost of what was in front of you a few thousandths of a second ago. How is this relevant to spiritual growth? In the illusion of a continual reality there are actually many gaps. We go away as much as we stay here. When you go away, blinking out of existence for a fleeting millisecond, you aren't anchored in physical reality. You voyage to the quantum dimension and beyond, for nobody knows exactly where the universe goes when it blinks on and off. But we do know certain things:

Physicality is an appearance created by the mind.
In its essence reality is invisible and intangible.
Events are ambiguous.
The only constant is change.
Radical uncertainty is at work all the time.

The exercise is to apply these truths to yourself. Instead of struggling to make life stable, unchanging, unambiguous, and certain, accept that you are a product of an uncertain, ambiguous creation. This isn't a flaw. It's the glory of the creative process to constantly flow and change. The more you can accept this, the easier it is to accept your own transformation.

Remind yourself of the following:

I am not fixed in time.
I am not fixed in space.
The person I think I am is actually a lingering memory.
The real me lies beyond the five senses.
I am participating in the flux of the cosmos at every instant.
The whole universe conspired to bring about this present moment.

In psychology there is a school of treatment known as cognitive therapy. It holds that a person's most powerful tool for change resides at the level of beliefs and assumptions. That is, we suffer because we have mistaken ideas about ourselves ("I don't deserve happiness," "Nothing ever works out"), and by clinging to these mistakes, we block reality. Therapy consists of replacing these wrong ideas with more realistic ones (for example, "I do deserve happiness," "Things have a way of working out"). The same is true in spiritual terms. If you replace mistaken ideas with correct ones, reality can replace illusion.

What makes this notion even more potent is that the mind creates both illusion and reality. You have a choice which one to invest in. Once you accept that you are constantly in flux, you are in a position to perceive the changeless ground of existence, the eternal Being that is the stage for eternal change.

14. *For where two or three are gathered in my name, I am there among them.*
Applying the teaching—Spiritual power increases as people gather together.

In every tradition people have worshipped together. In India, the word *Satsang* applies to such gatherings; the word implies truth that grows stronger because it is shared. In the Christian tradition, the word *communion* carries the same weight. Jesus is speaking for spirit or God when he says that he will be present whenever others gather in his name. To take him literally is to miss his point: Any group that communes in the name of spirit is effective, even when the name of Jesus isn't being evoked.

But what does it mean to say that spirit is present or that it grows stronger in a group? In group dynamics it's well-known that beliefs grow stronger when people gather. Dissent is discouraged and suppressed. Conformity becomes an increasing pressure. We tend to view this phenomenon as a threat, thanks to memories of extreme political and religious movements, but at a deeper level, what you and I accept as reality is always based upon an agreement we share. Reality isn't fixed; it isn't a given. Shared beliefs and perceptions form the raw material from which reality is made.

Therefore, when people gather together for spiritual growth, they make an agreement, silent or spoken, to become co-creators. To accomplish this, activity takes place at different levels:

New beliefs are expressed and accepted.
The mind accepts certain facts and rejects others.
A feeling of shared responsibility arises.
A new vocabulary is invented and adopted.
Bonding occurs at the emotional level.
At the subtle level, spirits align.

This whole complex of activity isn't confined to spiritual movements, although one definitely sees it at work in early Christianity. In the early Church, everything centered around two core beliefs: Jesus was the Messiah, and Jesus rose from the dead. These formed the basis of communion. Once the basis was set, the co-creators went on to build the immense edifice we call the Christian world.

At this moment, you have the same capacity to be a co-creator. All you need is a core belief: God-consciousness is attainable. When this belief is set in place, a group gathered together to achieve it can begin to build a new reality. In time it might become as immense as the Christian world. That part is unpredictable. At the very least, however, the spiritual power needed to reach God-consciousness will be increased many times over.

Exercise—Find others who share your aim to reach God-consciousness and gather together. I know this sounds daunting; it goes far beyond anything one could call an exercise. To commune with others involves commitment and a willingness to expose your deepest aspirations. It requires stepping out of conformity with society and finding souls you can align with, even if you have no other social ties. Many seekers choose not to meet these challenges. They attempt to walk the path in isolation, feeling suspicious of religious movements and shy about exposing their vulnerability in public.

I think a great deal of this reluctance can be overcome by discarding the model of religion. To gather together on the path isn't the same as forming a sect. There is no need for dogma, prayer, ritual, priests, or official scripture. No one is to be elevated above the rest. If the word *spiritual* connotes any or all of these negatives, you are conflating religious doctrine with spiritual growth. The two aren't the same, and we have an undeniable need to gather together for spiritual purposes.

My instinct is to follow the model of *Satsang,* which is a simple gathering for the purpose of speaking about truth. In church, people are included if they conform to a body of rules and beliefs. In *Satsang,* anyone can attend who has a love of spirit; there are no obligations because there is no official organization with an agenda. A *Satsang* can even be silent, or it can combine a period for meditation and a period for talking. In the form I prefer, one person is assigned to talk, another to comment, and then group discussion begins. There are no debates and rebuttals, no sermons, and no attempt to proselytize. The purpose is to let spirit expand, and words are useful only to that extent.

If this model appeals to you, it's easy to begin. Find one person and set aside a time when you can share your spiritual experiences. See if your vision is sympathetic to the vision of the other person. If so, then let the *Satsang* develop of its own accord. Bring in another member if you feel like it, or don't. Groups grow best when they grow spontaneously. You might choose to join a group that is already in existence, but be alert. If you begin to hear shared prejudices, fixed beliefs, a special vocabulary used by those in control, or any sign of proselytizing, move on. There are pitfalls in organized movements, yet this fact shouldn't negate how crucial it is to share the truth. By definition, the goal of God-consciousness is full inclusion.

15. What does it profit a man to gain the whole world if he loses his soul?

Applying the teaching—Keep your spiritual vision constantly in mind.

The scheme of the world has not changed since the time of Jesus. On one side are the claims of material existence: money, status, family, career, and so on. On the other side are the claims of spiritual life. Jesus made a sharp division between the two. He decried money and possessions; he even discounted work and family as incompatible with being on the spiritual path. The Church followed in his footsteps. Even though precious few Christians could literally give up every material tie in order to follow Christ, those who could became the ideal. By implication, those who couldn't felt they were falling short of the ideal.

I doubt that Jesus meant to be so exclusionary. He said explicitly that he had come for the fallen, the wayward, the lost sheep, the prodigal sons. All were included in his vision of a redeemed humanity. From this we can see that what matters is adhering to the vision, not whether you have a little or a lot in material terms. Jesus constantly uses the language of commerce to describe spiritual growth (profit and loss, building up treasure, storing up for winter). To me, this implies an acceptance that his listeners were firmly embedded in the material world and needed to be coaxed into a new world using their own language and values.

The situation remains the same today, and none of us is exempt. Our attachment to material goals overrides our ability to enter a new world. The solution comes down to having a vision and keeping it before your eyes. The world exerts constant pressure to conform to its values. Spirit exerts no pressure. This isn't a flaw. By its very nature growth is gradual, unseen, and effortless. But unlike a child, who doesn't have to remind himself to grow, a person on the spiritual path needs to keep reinforcing these new beliefs and values. The process is one of falling off the path and getting back on over and over, although I am reluctant to use a phrase like "falling off" when what occurs is more like being distracted or becoming forgetful. Your vision is a remedy for forgetfulness.

Exercise—This last exercise is open-ended. Sit and reflect upon your vision as it applies at this very moment. Consider what you want to achieve spiritually in the coming months or year. Now write down the most important things. For example, you might include the following:

Seeing God in everyone.
Finding communion with my family.
Feeling more compassionate.
Expressing love more freely.

Don't overload your list. It's best to pick a few things that are currently in the forefront of your inner life. If you are working on anger, for example, that's more important than something more removed and abstract, such as seeing God in everyone. At the same time, don't turn this into a list of spiritual chores. Include a few good things that are already blossoming in your life.

When you are satisfied with your list—and it needn't be long—
put it away for a day or two. Return to it to see if you still feel sin-
cerely and deeply that you have written down goals that mean the
most to you right now. Once you are satisfied, carry your list with
you in your wallet, or keep it in a drawer you open every day. Return
to it often. The aim here isn't to set an agenda but rather to remind
yourself to be attuned. Whenever you feel too much pressure from
worldly affairs, consult your list. Tell yourself that you are a spiritual creation in progress. You belong in the world but not of it. You
are using material life for a deeper purpose that isn't material. In
this way you can escape the notion that you are falling off the path
and getting on it again. The truth is more encouraging. You are living parallel lives that sometimes converge and sometimes separate.
As long as you keep your vision before you, the converging will
grow until the day comes when these parallel lines meet and become
one. You will embody your vision, and the world you see all around
you will reflect the unity of body, mind, and spirit.

HOW THE PATH OPENS

If we wanted to map the spiritual journey to God-consciousness, its contours would be different for each person. Nothing is more intimate and personal than your own awareness; we each relate to God on our own terms. But we can describe the general outlines of such a map.

The Beginning At the outset, our primary perception is of a huge chasm between ourselves and God. On this side of the abyss lie error and confusion, inner conflict and suffering. On the other side is the promise that all can be healed.

Jesus casts life as a struggle between good and evil, then, which is a dramatic way of portraying the spiritual chasm or abyss. The battle rages within as a struggle between one's demons and one's better angels.

Whether or not you accept this war as your own, the duality of darkness and light will shape your experience at the beginning of the path. On or off the path, everyone shares a deep longing for suffering to end, and yet we harbor a hopeless feeling that God has forgotten us, leaving us at the mercy of a random universe.

This yearning is fueled by the occasional glimpses that we catch of higher reality. The kinds of deeper experiences that are relevant cover a broad range, but they fall into a few simple categories: thinking, feeling, acting, saying, and being.

At any given moment a person might experience God on one of these levels, seemingly at random. Momentarily the gap between illusion and reality closes. The source of thinking, feeling, acting, and saying is consciousness, the ground state of existence. The fifth level, being, is consciousness itself without any mental activity. Following are some lists to help you recognize what it's like to shift your perception on each level. Some of these shifts may seem small and unrelated to God, but higher consciousness is achieved through many small steps until the entire perceptual field has changed.

Glimpses of Reality

Thinking:
Negative thoughts are replaced by positive ones.
The mind becomes calmer.
Thinking becomes clear and simple, clouds pass away.
Doubt gives way to certainty.
Obsessive and compulsive thoughts lose their grip.
Memory no longer haunts you with regrets.
You fantasize about the future less.
Solutions to problems appear more easily.

Feeling:
You feel more secure and positive about yourself.
You feel safe in the world.
You feel that you belong; you are no longer alone and isolated.

You are at ease, with less tendency to be overalert and vigilant.

You find yourself able to trust.

You sense a presence larger than yourself, and it feels close to you.

You feel lighter, less burdened.

Acting:

Activity becomes less chaotic.

You are no longer driven; external demands don't press in on you.

What you want to achieve comes more smoothly.

You find yourself no longer struggling.

You act more calmly, with less tendency to excitability or anxiety.

You interact with others more smoothly.

You stop acting on your inner fear, doubt, and anger.

You approach others with a sense of bonding connection rather than separation.

You act less aggressively; life is no longer a competition that pits "I, me, and mine" against "them."

Saying:

You start saying what is in your heart.

You speak from a center.

What you say is heard and paid attention to, respected.

You are more able to express love.

Your words are less defensive; you don't use them as a shield to protect your inner self.

You enjoy expressing yourself in a positive way.

You drop the habit of complaining and criticizing.

You are able to speak gently, and you are courteous from the level of the heart.

Being:

You sense a closeness to your true self.

You exist in peace with others.

You improve the atmosphere around you.
You enjoy just being here.
You catch glimpses of pure Being, or God.
"I am" is enough.
You have moments of sacred communion.

The Turning Point Into the state of the soul trapped in duality some light begins to shine. At the turning point a critical event shakes the soul. Everyday life is interrupted, either by a crisis or by a sudden epiphany, or by both, in what is described as "the dark night of the soul." For Christians this is the moment when a sinner sees the light, but the same imagery occurs in every spiritual tradition: The blind can see; the voice of God speaks; a holy presence descends; a heavy weight is lifted; rescue appears in the midst of danger; a loveless world radiates with love. It doesn't matter how many of these elements are present (and for some people it isn't even a personal experience, but an outside source of inspiration—a scripture or teacher—that convinces them of the existence of a higher reality). At this moment, something profound happens. It feels like being reborn, not simply because the old self drops away, but because the world itself shifts like a kaleidoscope. Your eyes register brighter colors, and a hidden light seems to be trying to break through the thin membrane of the world. Sounds become sweeter; nature seems to sing. Ordinary sensations acquire a delicious texture, like velvet or warm liquid, suffusing the body.

To an outsider the whole experience sounds dubious, like some kind of hallucination. But Jesus doesn't deny that this is the case; he just ascribes a different value to it. Salvation is a glimpse of reality; perception begins to detect illusion.

The Aftermath The astonishment of experiencing the turning point inevitably fades away. Descending back into mundane existence is very much like falling out of love. Your heightened perceptions return to their former state, which seems dull now. The presence of God withdraws; his voice grows silent. Love retreats from the world, leaving it as before. You have arrived at the aftermath of an epiphany.

Some people who have experienced the turning point respond by longing for a return to epiphany. When no amount of wishing, praying, or begging can bring it back, however, the aftermath can turn bleak or even desperate. The feeling of being deserted by God must be countered, but how?

Pray for God's presence.
Have faith that you aren't forgotten.
Read scripture to find a new way to live.
Imitate the model of Jesus.
Join with others in your position.
Renounce your old life and the ways of the world.
Surrender and worship.

I believe that the early Church was born in the aftermath of ecstasy, and its activity took just these forms. Just as you and I crave the return of a unique moment when our world turned to joy, the disciples of Jesus wanted him back. They couldn't have him back literally (although some believed that they could, a belief that turned into the Second Coming and the resurrection of the dead to meet Christ), but they could re-create the life they led with Jesus. In this way a wound was healed and a path opened up. When the divine presence is gone, only emptiness remains. The person can grieve this loss and remain bereft. That remains a strong temptation, as does the urge to lose oneself in nostalgic memories. The alternative is to look for some way to re-create the departed blessing. The most powerful thing that anyone can do, however, is to fill the void directly: going inward to find peace and silence; following the trail of spiritual clues; paying attention to the guidance of your soul; seeking your own essence; finding the presence of God; removing obstacles and inner resistance; changing your allegiance to the soul. I think nothing here is incompatible with Christian life. The aftermath is a precarious time, and some people don't strike out on their own; they are attracted to the safety and comfort of organized religion. Perhaps the prospect of an inner path feels too mystical or abstract. As an antidote to taking the easy way out, let's explore new responses as a way out of the aftermath.

Going inward—I am amazed at how many people do not choose this as their first response to the aftermath. They have had a glimpse of higher consciousness, but this gets translated into external activity, sometimes frantic activity. But if we look at this phenomenon more closely, the reason becomes obvious. Epiphanies are openings; many people experience them negatively. They feel a sense of turmoil inside that they want to shut down.

Turmoil is actually a positive sign; it's a symptom of spiritual ferment. In the aftermath, looking inward brings to light all the things we don't want to see. It's not peaceful or calming when we air out the unconscious mind. Fortunately, it doesn't have to be. There are natural mechanisms that can do the work of creating order out of chaos. Among other things, the soul stands for a permanent state of peace and order; these qualities increase when obstacles to the soul are removed. Light doesn't have to be created out of darkness, only allowed to shine.

Following the trail of spiritual clues—Turning points are real breakthroughs, and they set in motion a process of transformation. The higher self or soul leaves clues at every stage of the path. These come in many forms, but the surest way to recognize them is by contrast to one's former life. Glimpses of ecstasy appear, lasting only a moment or perhaps as long as a day. Fear and anxiety lift. You experience a certainty about being safe. Events fall into patterns instead of being random. Love seems like a presence in the world that carries its own strength. These are hints of the soul's reality.

Paying attention to the soul's guidance—Scattered clues wouldn't be enough to keep a seeker on the path. A path implies a sequence of events. In this case, since God-consciousness is an inner state, so are the events along the way. One experiences firsthand that ego and personality don't have to dominate one's life. The things they stand for—and tenaciously refuse to let go of—give way to a higher vision. As a model of God-consciousness, Jesus exhibited love, compassion, peace, humility, and intimate knowledge of spiritual truth. All these factors are far removed from the activity of the ego and personality, which focus on limited personal aims like money, possessions, social status, and all manner of hidden fears and anger.

The ego's stake in its own interests is so powerful, backed up by years of conditioning and inner propaganda, that we may only hear its voice warning us that trying to become spiritual will be disastrous. We will become vulnerable on every front, giving a free hand to fear, aggression, outside enemies, and irrationality. In a sense, this warning is correct, but only from the ego's point of view. Higher consciousness seems to spell the end of lower consciousness; therefore, it's logical for the status quo to fight hard against its own extinction.

The soul possesses another viewpoint. It knows that it is real, but also that it has no intention of annihilating the ego and the personality. Transformation isn't a war, and the soul never uses psychological violence. After all, no violence is required for a three-year-old child to grow into a four-year-old, with all the inner changes that implies. God-consciousness requires more inner change, yet it proceeds as spontaneously as a child learning to read. The chasm between literacy and illiteracy is huge; the two states have nothing in common, so we can't force one to turn into the other. We trust in the process of development, and the same holds true for spiritual growth. The more spontaneous it is, the more genuine.

Seeking your own essence—In the case of childhood development, it may seem that nothing is actually happening. If you make a video of a three-year-old's typical day, you won't see isolated moments of epiphany or awakening where the child says, "Aha, I just had a glimpse of what it will be like when I am four." Appearances are deceiving, however, because invisible changes are occurring beneath the surface, and when they come to fruition, the child will consciously know that something has happened. Old interests fall away; new ones arise. A stronger sense of confidence emerges, along with a more formed sense of self. What is the parallel in spiritual terms?

The soul is the highest form of the self. It doesn't unfold biologically like a child's brain and behavior. But in other respects there's an undeniable similarity: The soul works beneath the surface, and when its work comes to fruition, consciousness shifts. It would be wrong to say that children are the puppets of biology. They have to participate in their own development, taking an active interest in exploring the world and finding out their own potential. When this doesn't happen, when the child is inert and passive, the diagnosis is autism. In spiritual terms, the same holds true. The seeker must take an active interest in the soul's unfolding, or the result will be inert.

That's why I find myself reluctant to use the word *seeker,* because it denies the spontaneity of inner growth while at the same time implying that the goal is outside the self. Seekers seem like hunters on a safari to capture the soul. The spiritual path isn't like that. The goal is within and ever present. Better to say that one is trying to uncover the true essence of the self. We have all loved at times, felt compassion, and risen to acts of selflessness. This is the way the model of Jesus resonates with personal experience. We know the difference between being awake and asleep, at least vaguely, and being awake feels better. It produces a better life.

Despite all these glimpses of a higher existence, what we lack is continuity. Episodes come and go without taking us to a final, definitive change. The frog and the prince inhabit the same body. The only way to find consistency is to keep pursuing your own essence. You must keep in mind that the real you *is* love, *is* truth, *is* God. Even if you could manage the herculean task of imitating Jesus every moment of your life, unless you find your essence, the end result would be unreal. Fortunately, imitation isn't necessary. By removing the obstacles and resistances that hide your essence, you reveal yourself to yourself. Essence, being permanent, can't be destroyed, only masked. It patiently awaits the day when you wake up to who you really are.

Finding the presence of God—Invisible as the spiritual process is, it can't be totally beyond the senses. You must be able to feel the difference between progress and lack of it. The presence of the soul brings the presence of God. People report this in various ways: as a sense of lightness, inner joy, an unshakable peace of mind, and many other things. The experience is personal and fluid. But there needs to be something palpable to indicate that transformation is taking place.

Some of these indicators are fairly obvious. A person who sheds fear and anxiety knows that this is happening. When any negative aspect of yourself begins to improve, you are moving forward on the path. Yet it's equally true that the soul isn't your therapist. People make progress with their hidden anxiety and anger using Prozac and other psychotropic drugs far more than they make progress spiritually. The two areas have become blurred, in fact, to the extent that seeking God has become a kind of metatherapy. The aim is strictly to rid yourself of some inner discomfort like grief, addiction, or loneliness.

These are worthwhile goals, and certainly every means should be used to free yourself of inner pain. But that's not the same as finding your own essence. Something positive needs to grow. Most people crave the positive so much that they are easily fooled. They believe that a few doses of Jesus mixed with fervent prayer brings love and forgiveness. One hears about God's unconditional love from fundamentalists who live in deep denial about their own intolerance, hidden anger, and unfaced fears. This is not to point fingers. When the latest scandal hits the news about an evangelical preacher who has been hiding secret sins, the gap between righteous words and righteous actions becomes all too obvious. People who live in glass houses shouldn't throw scripture.

What's overlooked in these lurid moments is that inner obstacles are never easy to overcome entirely. The process always follows a rhythm of give and take, forward and backward. Jesus can't be expected to lift sin all at once. But gradually, sin—the guilty knowledge of being imperfect, of doing wrong and falling short of your best self—gives way to righteousness, the happy knowledge that your best self exists and is emerging. In the mixture of perfection and imperfection lies ordinary human existence.

Removing obstacles and inner resistance—The give-and-take that everyone experiences on the path isn't the result of the soul coming and going. The soul's presence is constant; what wavers is our perception of it. Why does it waver? To the devoutly religious, the answer tends to be moral: We are all sinners who fall into temptation. In terms of consciousness, however, the moral dimension—along with the guilt and shame it produces—isn't where we turn first. First we examine the mind, where many kinds of obstacles exist. When the mind is in a state of resistance, obstacles hide the presence of the soul. In practical terms, the time spent on the path is devoted to finding your own inner resistance and gradually melting it away. The give-and-take with God is an illusion; the real give-and-take is with your own awareness.

This is where being a child of God isn't the same as being a child. When a toddler learns to walk, one can't say that walking was present already. Spiritual growth is accelerated by experience. Thirty years ago, the EEGs of people as they sat in meditation proved that brain waves were being altered, with an increase in alpha waves. Now researchers can verify that after prolonged periods of meditation, such as the years spent in monasteries by Tibetan Buddhist monks, the so-called hard wiring of the brain may undergo permanent changes. Primarily, the centers that light up on MRIs when a person faces sudden stress don't react in long-term meditators. The neurological centers for anger, anxiety, alarm, and reflexive fight-or-flight appear to be quiescent. In this way the physical correlates for "the peace that passeth understanding" can actually be observed.

That said, the spiritual path shouldn't be mistaken for dulling the brain. Jesus speaks of waking up, which implies increased alertness inside. The experience of essence is subtle. If it weren't, we would all be aware of having it already. By facing our own limitations, a process of expansion begins as old boundaries dissolve. We know this isn't an illusion of brain chemistry, because as resistance vanishes, hidden possibilities unfold. Suddenly a person can feel love and express it. Insights reveal new truths about the self and about life. In other words, your existence becomes more meaningful. That's the most reliable guide to inner growth, not the arrival of peace by itself or even the departure of personal demons. Those are important changes, but unless meaning blossoms as your vision deepens, the only change that has occurred inside is healing.

Changing your allegiance to the soul—Once you have enough indications that the spiritual path is real and that you belong on it, a radical shift can take place. You shift your allegiance from the ego to the soul. This isn't the same as becoming holy overnight. It doesn't require you to drop everything that isn't spiritual. Something more subtle is involved, closer to entering a silent contract, perhaps.

From birth, we have all been locked into a contract with the ego. Our lives are dominated by "I, me, and mine." Now the terms of this contract are undergoing a profound change.

To some extent the limits of language make it difficult to describe this shift. "Small self" and "lower self" imply negative value judgments. The experience that words can't touch is of boundaries expanding and a limited sense of self dropping away. The ego can't accomplish these changes, and as long as your deepest allegiance is given to your ego, they won't occur; you will be tantalized by the prospect of freedom but find yourself unable to walk out of prison.

Jesus was a simple teacher who brought the hidden reality of the soul down-to-earth. He understood that naturalness and simplicity are touchstones of wisdom.

Keeping It Simple

Appreciate your experiences, but don't try to own them.

Avoid thinking of the path as "my" path.

Let things come and go without attachment.

Don't pretend to be more positive than you actually feel.

Don't exaggerate your experiences, to yourself or others.

Share your path only with someone you trust.

Offer thanks with simplicity.

Don't allow your experiences to set you apart from or above anyone else.

Don't be tempted to think you are a saint.

If you examine the life of Jesus, he practiced all of these things, to the point of pushing away anyone who fawned over him. He distanced himself from his own miracles and lived with exemplary humility. Yet at the same time, his state of God-consciousness was so exalted that it changed history. One of the glories of the Christian legacy, in fact, is the striking dichotomy between Jesus's humility and his exaltation.

I'm aware that some spiritual teachers depict the rise to higher consciousness as a struggle, sometimes of heroic proportions; in fact, they hold that "ego death" offers the only hope for progress. Is this Jesus's view? The gospels have him warning against Satan, often called "the evil one." But far more often Jesus directs his followers away from struggle. He speaks of simple faith being enough to carry someone to Heaven. He talks of redemption through God as a matter of asking and automatically receiving.

Jesus himself renounced Satan during his time in the wilderness. This episode has been called upon as evidence that fighting against the devil should be a major focus of Christian life: If Jesus had to steel himself against temptation, how can things be any different for us? Matthew, Mark, and Luke all contain descriptions of Christ's temptation, which is a critical episode because by renouncing the evil one, Jesus refused to accept dominion over the world in material terms. Not only does it take the Messiah to be offered the chance to rule the world, it takes the Messiah to resist it.

As told in Mark, widely considered the original for Matthew and Luke, Jesus had just been baptized by John the Baptist. The Holy Spirit had descended "like a dove on him. And a voice came from heaven, 'You are my Son, the Beloved; with you I am well pleased.'" (Matthew 1:10–11) Immediately, Jesus is led by the spirit to go out into the wilderness (or desert) "tempted by Satan; and he was with the wild beasts, and the angels waited on him."

In other words, the moment God showed that Jesus was his own, Satan made a claim from the other side. This was a contest for Jesus's allegiance. We are reminded of the wager that God and Satan made over the soul of Job in the Old Testament, yet another mythic reminder that would help him qualify as the Messiah. Matthew offers much more detail than the bare skeleton in Mark's account. He has Jesus fasting for forty days while the devil tries to strike a bargain with him.

First the tempter offers bread to the famished Jesus, who responds with, "It is written, 'One does not live by bread alone, but by every word that comes from the mouth of God.'" (Matthew 4:3) The devil is famous for quoting scripture for his own purpose, and he does that next. He flies Jesus to the highest point of the temple in Jerusalem and dares him to jump: "For it is written, 'He will command his angels concerning you,' and, 'On their hands they will bear you up, so that you will not dash your foot against a stone.'"

We can see that the gospel writer has concocted this battle of quotation for the usual reason, one that he was fixated on: To be the real Messiah, Jesus had to fulfill all the old prophecies. And so it continues. To the second temptation, Jesus replies, "Again it is written, 'Do not put the Lord your God to the test.'" As his final offer, Satan takes Jesus to a mountaintop and shows him the kingdoms of the world spread out below, saying, "All these I will give you, if you will fall down and worship me." But Jesus remains true to the role assigned to him and quotes another scripture: "Away with you, Satan! for it is written, 'Worship the Lord your God, and serve only him.'" Then the devil left him, and suddenly angels came and waited on him. Compared to Mark, who compresses the devil's temptation and the angels waiting on Jesus into one sentence, one has the feeling that Matthew spliced in the details because he had a point to make, and this was the right place to do it.

The point is to link Jesus inexorably to Jewish tradition. He spends forty days in the desert to echo the forty-day flood that Noah endured. The desert location itself mirrors the wandering of the Israelites after Moses led them from captivity in Egypt. Besides looking backward, however, the temptation of Christ looks forward as well, setting a pattern for countless believers, including the purest saints, who feel tempted to stray from Jesus into the arms of sin.

The episode in the desert can be seen just as credibly—and much more universally—as a test between the material world, dominated by ego, and the world of the soul, dominated by spirit. Most Christians are unaware that centuries before in India, the king of the demons, Mara, came to tempt Buddha under the Bodhi tree. Their encounter is equally mythic. It occurs on the night when Siddhartha, a prince who became a seeker, finally attains enlightenment. Mara offers Siddhartha the same rulership of the world that Satan did to Jesus, but he also mocks Siddhartha's claim to deserve to be enlightened. He manifests threatening illusions, including a parade of war elephants and swarms of demons. Even Mara's three beautiful daughters are thrown into the bargain. Buddha was able to see through the illusory nature of these blandishments, just as Christ was able to say, "Satan, get thee behind me."

In our own lives, the model of the temptation of Christ doesn't reflect the reality of transformation. It's not productive to feel that you are being tempted by the devil or that sin is the correct term for aspects of human nature. I'm thinking about a personal experience that I found troubling and poignant at the same time. At the height of the scandal over Catholic priests abusing children in Boston, I was asked to comment on CNN. I drove to the studio knowing that judgment had already been leveled against the priests who had violated their vows, and the law, by sexually preying on young boys. And yet no one had commented on the fact that two worlds were clashing, which was the real root of the problem.

On the one hand, we have the secular world and the rule of law. On the other hand, we have the Christian world and the rule of God. In the Christian world pedophilia is a grave sin. The person who commits it has offended God and must seek forgiveness, which will be granted through Christ, because no sin is so grievous that it cannot be forgiven. Yet this notion of forgiveness outrages most people, since in the secular world pedophilia is a crime, and whoever commits it deserves to be punished to the full extent of the law. Thinking about this, I was strongly tempted to turn the car around and miss the TV interview, because I couldn't see how these two worlds could be reconciled. To accept the totally secular view would be giving up on mercy. We are all imperfect, and none of us could endure life without hope of forgiveness. Much less could we tolerate having our psychological defects labeled a crime punishable to the full extent of the law.

On the other hand, the Catholic Church was being entirely unrealistic not to acknowledge the psychological dimension of child abuse. Spirituality cannot be a refuge for warped psyches. One imagines a young gay male turning to the priesthood to save himself from shameful feelings and urges he doesn't understand. Instead of being a salvation, however, his decision leads only to more repression, secrecy, and shame. Years go by, and he finds that the same urges exist; worse still, they are directed at the same age group he fantasized about at the age of twelve or thirteen, a confusing time when attraction to the same sex isn't always a marker of homosexuality. The price for turning to God is that no "cure" has taken place, either psychologically or spiritually.

Eventually I did go into the studio, but the instant I raised the possibility of two worlds being in conflict, the host's face turned ashen. He leaned into his microphone and said, "Of course, you're not condoning what these priests did in any way, right?" I could tell that he was trying to rescue me from a disastrous slipup. I replied, "No, I am not condoning them. The law must take its course," after which the host switched to another, less explosive question.

In hindsight, I see that what was nagging at me was the whole issue of allegiance we've been discussing. Our divided psyches haven't answered the vital question, "Where do I belong, in the material world or the world of the soul?" People who want to be close to God often feel that they are being tested every day to see if they will commit a sin. Some even worry that having sinful thoughts is enough to throw them into the hands of Satan. In the secular world the word *sin* may not apply, but guilt pushes us away from the soul anyway, because people are haunted by a sense that they don't deserve to be on the spiritual path.

So strong is the grip of temptation in the Christian sense that some believers turn it into their own personal drama. On an evangelical broadcast, I once watched the account of a man who was climbing a peak in the Swiss Alps. He had arrived high above the tree line, looking out on a vast, empty expanse of mountains, when suddenly he realized that the devil was after him. Demons appeared out of nowhere, descending upon him with howls and gnashing teeth. In the distance, the man saw a wayside chapel of the kind familiar in the Alps. He ran toward it, desperately calling out to Jesus. Fortunately, he reached safety in the nick of time, and as he fell to his knees before the crucifix, he felt Christ's presence. As in the gospels, Christ ordered Satan and his minions to leave, and instantly they did.

Can anyone tell this man that he created his life-and-death scenario in his mind? The demons who pursued him were conjured up from his own images of the Christian struggle between good and evil. Vivid images lurked in his memory, placed there by things he first heard, no doubt, in Sunday school. Neurologists inform us that the strongest glue of any memory is emotion. That's why you can remember the time your mother lost track of you in the supermarket or the first step you took onto the school bus. Anxiety impressed the memory in your mind, while events with little emotional significance, like the car your neighbor drove when you were ten, fade away.

There's no doubt that the war between sin and salvation carries powerful emotions with it. Has there ever been a more powerful story than the life of Jesus? Buddha and Lao-tzu have nothing to compare with it, and the military adventures of Muhammad, replete with narrow escapes in the night and pitched battles, don't have the sweetness and emotional depth of Jesus's arc from miraculous birth to tragic sacrificial death. By comparison, the path to God-consciousness lacks drama. How can a mere process compete with the spectacle of Jesus's life?

Yet emotion isn't a reliable guide in this case. The most important activity of the mind isn't the war between good and evil. It's the sifting of real from unreal. Consciousness is the field where all thoughts, images, and words are born. The ones that foster illusion jostle against those that reveal reality. Jesus says as much in his own words on the occasions when he warns against the illusion of the material world. We need to remember that. His teaching is all about choosing to align yourself with God because he alone is real.

THE MIDDLE OF THE JOURNEY

In the middle of the journey one begins to reap the fruits of spiritual life. As turmoil lessens and the soul comes closer, profound shifts occur. Epiphanies are no longer sudden bursts of ecstasy. Relating to yourself as a spiritual being becomes more constant and subtle.

"I took meditation very seriously in my twenties," a friend told me who has been on the path for thirty years. "I went so far as to move into a spiritual community where the routine was to get up at dawn and meditate for several hours, repeating this for several more hours in the afternoon when we came home from work. I loved the life. People make fun of that word, but anyone who has gone deep enough into silence to experience bliss knows how seductive and appealing it is. I felt that I had found my peace.

"A lot of other things were going on. My ego kicked up a lot of junk I didn't want to face; I discovered that beneath my niceness, which always seemed positive to other people, I was harboring anger and resentment. My mind was like a glass of water that had a layer of mud at the bottom. Before I moved into the community, my mind seemed clearer than it did afterward. The mud had settled to the bottom, leaving clear water above it. Now the mud was beginning to stir, and the whole thing looked cloudy. Yet over time this changed. Bliss was the reward, as I saw it, for doing the hard work of cleaning the mud out."

There are many different images for the process of spiritual growth. If you ask people what's going on, the range of responses is wide:

I'm getting in contact with God.

I'm living from the level of the soul.

I don't have as much attachment to my ego.

I'm finding my own truth.

There's more love in my life, and I'm able to receive it better.

I'm changing my old conditioning and addictions.

I'm beginning to feel new again.

Now I can remember who I really am.

One of these descriptions might relate to your own journey. Yet it's not possible to feel that you're growing every minute. There are times when no growth seems to be happening, when you've lost your focus. You experience discouraging setbacks, and long stretches where you've reached a plateau and can't seem to move beyond it. The middle of the journey is a period of rewards and frustrations.

There is no one way to describe the middle of the journey. The important thing is not to be misled by its ups and downs. I was struck by the story of a very experienced teacher who had become well versed in Sufism, the mystical path of Islam. He had achieved many remarkable things spiritually, until one day the light vanished.

"I was sitting at the breakfast table with my wife, when the thought occurred to me, Who is that? I love my wife deeply, but at that moment I felt I was looking at a stranger. I tried to shake the feeling, but without success. For a long time it was quite baffling, because I had assumed that I was making steady progress toward reaching God.

"Then I realized what was happening. It's like this: You work for years to climb the mountain. You're nearly at the summit, and you see God's hand reaching down for you. Eagerly you run toward it, and just as your fingers are about to touch his, God says, 'Have you forgotten something?' It's a shock, because you realize at that moment that you made the summit by leaving behind all the parts of yourself that you hate and are ashamed of. You didn't plan to take your secrets with you to meet God, but that's how it is. You must go back down and find the orphans and abandoned children crying in the dark. Not just your best self finds God. All of you does."

Everyone meets resistance on the spiritual path, and future success depends a great deal on facing and overcoming the obstacles you encounter. Let's go into this in detail.

Why You Resist Spirit

Habit—The new experience doesn't fit your way of doing and thinking. Your mind is conditioned to cling to its old ways and resists change.

Memory—Your past overshadows the present. You assume that you already know what life has to offer.

Guilt—You draw back from new experience because you harbor a secret sense of past sins.

Self-worth—You feel that you don't deserve these new experiences. They are "too good" for someone like you.

Repressed anger, sorrow, and grief—Old emotions that you have never fully released begin to surface. This frightens you, and you feel like shoving them back down into their hiding place.

Loss of control—The new experience causes inner turmoil and conflict. It feels as if you aren't in control anymore, which creates panic.

Skepticism and doubt—You don't believe that your experiences are real because your rational mind refuses to accept them.

Victimization—You are accustomed to disappointing others and have very low expectations. You expect something bad to come out of any experience, no matter how good it may seem at the moment.

This may seem like a formidable array of obstacles standing in your way, but in practice you don't have to take heroic measures to overcome them. Once more, simplicity is the key. When any negative feeling or reaction to a situation arises, stop to notice it, just as you would with a positive feeling, and make a choice about what to do. The choices cover a wide range of responses. At any given moment you will need to experiment a bit to find the one that seems most suitable. The following can be very effective:

Patient waiting—Notice your negative reaction and watch it for a moment. Be attentive to your feelings as they are, without judging or forcing them to change. This response is quiet, but it isn't passive. You are removing the shock value of the moment, softening the feeling so that you don't act on it impulsively or push it away. You are letting it dissipate naturally, at its own pace. You are also practicing detachment. These are all deep spiritual responses.

Talk out the problem—Any negative experience in the mind is part of yourself. It's neither alien nor evil. Try talking to your fear or hostility. Ask to know what it means. Find out why it chose to show itself at this particular moment. Address your negativity respectfully but without fear. You have no cause for fear, because as unwelcome as any negative experience might be, you are seeing a fragmented aspect of yourself, something you overlooked or hid away. Because it feels like a part of you, your anger, fear, or any other negative aspect wants you to heal it. This can happen only through understanding. So talking out your negative feelings with yourself can be very helpful. It brings to the surface whatever you are supposed to look at.

Ask the underlying energy to leave—Not all negativity wants to stick around. We are all aware of passing moods and sudden flashes of emotion that soon subside. Ask the negative energy to leave, but first give it a chance to say what it has to say. If you begin to think of fear, anger, anxiety, worry, and other negative responses as messages rather than afflictions, they become less "sticky." They begin to lose their obsessive, insistent quality. When you really explore the shadow, you find that energy is stuck to a message. The energy captures your attention; the message has something to say. Both parts need to be understood. If you try to get rid of fear and anger without knowing their meaning, they will grow stronger and return. If you get the message but don't work on dispelling the energy it is stuck to, negative feelings will persist. But by listening to the message and then moving the energy, you can free yourself even of the most persistent negative reactions.

Summon help and assistance—Your mind has countless levels. At higher levels, you possess much more control and authority than you realize. Learning to trust in aspects of your higher self that you can't see is important. Ask for help in removing unwanted negative energy. Some people address their angels and guides; others pray to God; still others make a request to the higher self directly. Depending on your own beliefs, don't hesitate to say that you are feeling overwhelmed and need help.

Physical responses—Turn to the wisdom of the body. Although the mind always wants to rush in and take charge, life is a cooperative venture between mind and body. As some body workers like to say, there are issues in the tissues. So let your body do what it wants in order to release the grip of a negative experience. You probably know already if you are the sort of person who gets rid of stress by walking or by going to the gym. Many other kinds of bodily movements are helpful. I know people who allow themselves to shake, tremble, thrash their limbs, and so on. This is their exorcism dance.

Others use toning, which means humming or singing at a certain pitch and then letting the body carry the tone up or down. The process is simple. Lie on your back in a comfortable position and begin to hum or sing a tone. Which one doesn't matter. It can be high or low, loud or soft. Go inward and relax. Let the tone do what it wants. Many people find that high pitches help clear fuzziness or dullness in the head; repetitive thoughts and worries can be toned out this way. Lower, growling tones seem to work best in the abdomen. But these are just general guides.

Toning must be suited to a person's immediate situation, and that can happen only through experience. The first step is always the same. Lie still, start to tone, and see where it takes you. The presence of a continuous tone seems to smooth the release of stuck energies. Laughter and tears work well for almost everyone, for opposite reasons. Laughter has a tonic effect, while crying expresses the underlying sorrow that is part of most negative energies. We tend to think of laughing and crying as emotional responses, but they have strong physical effects as well.

Breathing—Your breathing changes in rate and depth according to how relaxed you are and what your mental state is. In many spiritual traditions the breath is also a subtle connection to higher realities, bringing in life energy from the source. It can be helpful to use some kind of controlled breathing to let go of unwanted negative energies. Here are two simple exercises:

1. Lie flat on your back in bed or on a thick carpet. Spread your feet and place your hands out away from your body so that you are in an open position. Take easy, regular breaths, not counting or timing them. Feel your out-breath carrying away negative energies in a

gentle stream. When you feel relaxed enough, begin to yawn. Allow your yawn to reach deep. Feel your body as it gets ever more relaxed; keep yawning several more times, then lie quietly for a few minutes. If you happen to doze off, don't resist.

2. Lie in the same open position as above. After a moment, take a deep sigh, reaching down into your abdomen as deep as the sigh can go. Then release all at once, allowing the breath to *whoosh* out of its own accord, without using your chest muscles to force it out. Wait a moment before repeating. Ask each deep sigh to release any energies that want to go at that moment. After six to ten sighs, lie quietly for a while. If you begin to doze off, don't resist.

We've covered a fairly large repertoire of simple techniques. It takes time before you find the right response to suit a specific situation. Remain flexible; be aware that no single technique works all the time. The more patient you are with yourself, the better. One day you may need tears, the next day it's a matter of patient waiting or talking to your inner self. The goal isn't to empty out these old residues as fast as possible, but to relate to them in a new way. Instead of rejecting the fragments of experience that you fear and dislike, you are owning them as part of yourself, to be treated with as much respect as you treat yourself.

You will also find it helpful to know the kind of response that *doesn't* work.

Rationalizing —Don't dismiss your negativity as simply a mood. Don't tell yourself you don't have time for this kind of response or that it's insignificant. If a hidden fragment of yourself has come to the surface after being submerged for months or years, the event is significant.

Ego—When you have feelings you don't happen to approve of, don't say, "This doesn't happen to someone like me," or "I'm not that kind of person." Inside, you are reflections of the whole world.

This fact is a huge blessing, but not from your ego's viewpoint. Ego wants to recognize only those experiences that bolster its belief in I, me, and mine. When an experience arises that diminishes the ego, it gets rejected. If an unwanted feeling or situation really touches a nerve, the ego responds more violently, resorting to stronger and stronger rejection and judgment, repression, and denial. Yet these tactics are the very obstacles that you need to remove. They serve only to make you numb and unresponsive.

Timidity and fear—Negative energies are always connected to memory, because they are the residue traces of past experience. These residues come out with shadows of the way they came in. That's why, when confronting old anger or fear, you will often see images from the past and resurrect long-buried emotions. It's tempting to react timidly and withdraw from these. Remember that you are not the same person you were in the past, so it's not necessary to react as if you are still a child. Back then, you weren't equipped to face loss, grief, anxiety, and loneliness. What you are experiencing now, as these memories discharge their energy, is only a shadow, not the real thing.

Procrastination—Negative energies rarely pick just the right moment to emerge, but you shouldn't tell yourself that you will look at them tomorrow instead of today. Tomorrow, they will be only a memory; you won't be confronting the real essence of what's inside you. There's one exception, however. If your negativity comes up because of another person, don't discharge toward them. They are only triggering what has been inside you all along. Wait to confront your negativity until you are alone. This requires you to take responsibility for how you feel. The easy way out is to externalize your negative energy by blaming someone else and making that person the target of your emotions. It's harder but more productive to face the truth that all our negative energy belongs to us, not to someone else. On that assumption, you can heal what you own to be yours.

Spiritual Mood Swings

What feels like backsliding in the middle of the journey is actually a return to parts of yourself that need spiritual attention. The soul is constant; only your perception changes. You see yourself leaping forward or falling back. You find inner peace only to lose it again. You struggle to overcome discouragement and the temptation to reclaim the normal life you had before this whole seduction of spirit lured you in.

It's helpful to prepare yourself for these spiritual mood swings and to learn how to react to them. A woman who had spent years practicing yoga and meditation spoke to me in a bitter mood: "I spent all this time renouncing the world, and what did I get? Older. Out of touch with my family. And probably very weird. I don't mean to be crass, but where's the payoff?" She had cut her ties with a famous Indian guru and was working as an office temp. I asked her if she had noticed any signs of spiritual progress. After all, she had devoted herself intensely to her practices.

"I got a night-light out of it," she said ironically. "That's what I call this blue shimmer that I see in my sleep. My body goes to sleep at night, but my mind remains alert, and there's a faint blue light that goes with that."

Since she had asked my opinion, I said, "Do you know what this night-light, as you call it, really is? You are witnessing your own awareness. You are awake inside even when your body is asleep. You've arrived at the source of the mind, and that's a huge accomplishment. The fact that you're dissatisfied is important to you right now, but that doesn't take away from your accomplishment."

She looked confused. She wasn't used to thinking that hers was a success story. "We tell ourselves all kinds of stories on the path," I said. "And what they all have in common is that they're never completely true. When you refer to yourself as 'I,' who is that person? The 'I' when you were three years old or the 'I' on your wedding day? The 'I' who found a vision to live by or the 'I' who now feels that her vision can't be attained?" I asked.

Every self is provisional. "I" is temporary and subject to everything that time brings: One day it was born, and one day it will die. The ego shifts constantly. We experience this whether we're on the path or not. "Most people don't see a way out of life's uncertainty," I told this woman. "Their spiritual house stands on sand. Yours doesn't. You've actually built something you can rely on, no matter how many ups and downs you go through."

No matter whether "I" feels victorious or defeated, elated or discouraged, these are mere phantoms compared to consciousness itself. Out of consciousness everything else is built. The world consists of images on a screen, and consciousness is the steady light that emanates from the projector. As I talked, the woman began to soften a little and asked me why she was experiencing such drastic uncertainty. How could she be so certain of her soul one day and so unsure the next?

"Because your old sense of self isn't going to give up so easily," I said. It would be tidier if spiritual seeking were just a matter of enduring one dark night of the soul, after which you would feel secure in your link to God. But there are many dark mornings of the soul, many shadowy afternoons and dim twilights. The middle of the journey concerns all the things Jesus taught his disciples about reaching God-consciousness.

Fear—When Jesus holds out a vision of the Kingdom of God, he is promising a place without fear, and he opens a way to reach that place. In the Kingdom of God this most basic need is fulfilled. If you begin your journey with a great deal of fear, God is far away. He has abandoned you or isn't listening. He may be punishing you with guilt, physical hardship, or abuse. If the difficulties in your life are external (lack of money, no job, isolation from other people), God will also feel external, a harsh judge manipulating the world to your disadvantage, loading the dice against you. On the other hand, if your troubles are more internal (anxiety, depression, guilt), God also moves inward. He becomes the punishing voice in your head, the superego constantly criticizing you. Nothing you do is ever good enough. You deserve to be a victim because of your sins.

On the spiritual path fear must be confronted. You must begin to see, layer by layer, that all fears are self-created. But when we speak of layers, it's not that fear is like coats of paint. Fear becomes enmeshed in the self; it feels like "me." This "me" feels real; its anxieties are very convincing. As long as that's true, more reasons to live in fear will crop up. The fear you harbor is like a video projector generating images of things to be afraid of, and even if you run out of images, there is free-floating anxiety to contend with. Advancement on the spiritual path can be measured in many ways, but a steady decrease in fear is the best.

Love—In the space where fear once lived, love enters to replace it. The Kingdom of God contains only love. Anything that falls short of this ideal hasn't been fully transformed. In Jesus's eyes, the everyday world feebly reflects divine love. This holds the key to one of his most disturbing teachings:

> If anyone comes to Me, and does not hate his own father and
> mother and wife and children and brothers and sisters, yes, and
> even his own life, he cannot be My disciple.
>
> *(Luke 14:26)*

Jesus seems to be ordering his disciples to abandon every cherished relationship, yet this makes no sense from a teacher who also commands them to love their enemies. As we've seen so often, Jesus speaks in absolutes to catch his listener's attention, and here he is making the sharpest possible distinction between ordinary love and divine love. "Me" stands for God, and "coming to Me" means entering the Kingdom of God, which is to say, God's reality. That reality isn't physical; it isn't found in worldly relationships, even the most loving ones. If you want to know divine love, you must find it on its own terms, not the terms you are used to.

Even when phrased more softly, this is a radical teaching. A person doesn't start with everyday love and then direct that feeling toward God. A complete reversal of perception is necessary—to dramatize this reversal, Jesus turns the word *love* into *hate*.

Elsewhere Jesus offers an easier path, when he says that his followers should love the Father. By using the familiar word *father*, which appears innumerable times in the gospels, divine love and earthly love seem similar. But the mystical Jesus regards the entire world as an illusion, which would make the love we experience here also an illusion. Now the word *hate* becomes understandable; Jesus is warning us off the kind of unreal love that lulls us, blinding us to God's love. Everyday earthly love is unreal because it fluctuates—it comes and goes, other people can take it from us. Everyday love depends upon pleasure; when we dislike the person who loves us, love wanes. If the one we love betrays us, love disappears altogether.

By contrast, divine love has no attachment and no conditions— the beloved doesn't have to be faithful or beautiful to bring pleasure or make you feel wanted. Divine love is the presence of the light. It fills every corner of creation with the same intensity. On the spiritual path, therefore, you shift your expectations. No longer is your family a model for love. Only love generated directly by the light is worthy of the name. Yet in the end, when God-consciousness is reached, exceptions no longer hold. The closer you come to God, the more you love everything, because his creation has become your creation.

The Kingdom of God is pure light, the source of love in its infinite variety. The journey to this place begins with a longing to experience love at its most intense. Christian saints speak of being shattered by God's love, burned to ashes, torn limb from limb by it.

Romans in the late pagan era were sophisticated, worldly people who adhered to the forms of religion without needing anything more. They were astonished at the Christian martyrs who were in such bliss that they sang hymns while being torn apart by wild beasts or attacked by gladiators.

In the middle of the journey, moments of ecstasy appear, along with periods of being surrounded by love in all directions. Such episodes occur in every life; it's not necessary to see yourself on the spiritual path. But the path is about such moments; it provides focus and direction so that love can expand, filling in the blank spaces where it is lost sight of. You announce your intention to reach the Kingdom of God, and in response, God's love steadily draws you closer.

Presence and fullness—Compared to the Kingdom of God, the material world is empty because it lacks God's presence. Presence (which Gnostics called *Pleroma,* the Greek word for "fullness") generally refers to the totality of God's powers. To be in the presence of God isn't like entering a throne room to bow before a king, although that is how many devout Christians might imagine it. Nor is it a warm glow that signals God's attention being turned on you, although that is how some Christian mystics describe it. Presence is all-encompassing; it includes both good and evil.

For us, the middle of the journey is about blurring the line dividing the world in two. Gradually wholeness emerges, and that wholeness is God's presence. Since our minds operate in duality, however (separating darkness and light, good from evil), God's fullness poses a problem: Nobody is special in God's presence. It makes us uncomfortable to believe that God is like the rain that falls on the just and unjust alike. We don't want to believe that he is as present in a sinner as in a saint.

Jesus himself needed to find a way to communicate God's omnipresence to an audience that could comprehend only stark distinctions, with God, the law, and Heaven on one side and Satan, chaos, and Hell on the other. Sometimes he used the symbol of a king ruling the whole world. Other times he resorted to mystification, saying that God's reality is unimaginable. The basic question is how to experience a state of wholeness with a mind that is divided and fragmented and a brain that's hardwired to make distinctions.

The way out of this dilemma isn't through finding the right words or even the right idea. Words and ideas belong to the active mind. God's presence belongs to consciousness. Jesus confounded the priests when he said, "Before Abraham, I am," because they didn't understand that "I" was transcendent; it didn't refer to a person. One of the reasons that the Crucifixion was inevitable is that it proved Jesus had no stake in the world. He was willing to give away the very thing—his life—that people wanted God to protect. In our terms, he was proving that to be enlightened means you no longer have a personal stake in the world.

In the middle of the journey we exchange our material wishes, fears, hopes, and dreams for a single, undisturbed state. In that state change is secondary, nonchange is primary. What does nonchange feel like? As with everything else, there are many descriptions depending on who is doing the describing. The easiest way, however, is to point to the aspects of change that begin to subside:

The mind stops being frantic, restless, and obsessed.
The threat of sin and evil decreases.
God stops being a person, either benign or threatening.
Attachment to material things lessens.
"Us vs. them" thinking stops being so appealing.
There is less need for self-importance. At the other extreme,
    there is less need to see oneself as a victim.
Issues of social status, money, and possessions no longer
    seem so important.

Love is less confined to people who love you back or
who occupy your sexual fantasies.

At the most general level, the self doesn't feel so constrained. Boundaries of every kind begin to disappear. Such boundaries exist so that you can control your life, censor it, and shut out aspects of reality that make you too uncomfortable.

Psychologically, only a fraction of the feelings, sensations, thoughts, and possibilities that reach the mind ever get to enter it. The rest are shunted aside through the mechanisms of denial, repression, and rejection. Denial says, "If I don't see it, it doesn't exist." Repression says, "If I hide it deep enough, it doesn't exist." Rejection says, "If I dismiss it angrily enough, it doesn't exist." After a lifetime of perfecting these mechanisms—and make no mistake, even the most open, tolerant person has honed them to a fine degree—the window that God can enter through is very tiny. Realizing this, Jesus speaks of God (and himself) as a thief sneaking into a house at night when the owner is asleep.

The middle of the journey opens the window one inch at a time, but however gradual the process, the ego resists it. The whole scheme of "I, me, mine" depends upon creating a stronghold for the ego. This struggle to maintain protection and isolation is considered totally necessary in the childhood stage of ego development. Without knowing where your boundaries begin and end, you would be autistic, bleeding into the world and other people. Or if you didn't reach that extreme, you would drift without direction, unable to define your own focus in life.

In this regard, however, the ego has made a mistake. Boundaries are necessary at the most basic level of the self, but as soon as a person becomes psychologically attached to them, freedom is lost. The door that keeps God out also keeps the self locked in. The word *prison* occurs 143 times in the Bible, all of them in the literal sense.

More than half of these references occur in the New Testament. When Jesus comes to share this experience, he transforms it. He undergoes physical imprisonment only to ascend to Heaven. He liberates himself from the tomb to transcend death. Therefore, when he teaches his disciples that the truth will make them free, layers of meaning are at work. They will be free from political persecution, religious intolerance, physical limitations, and eventually death itself.

Freedom is all-encompassing; it brings you into God's presence by releasing you from the illusion that you live behind walls. The ego could never succeed in its project of keeping reality outside the gate and admitting only a fraction of experience. Boundaries are fictions, convenient for the ego's purposes but ultimately not real. In the middle of the journey it dawns on us that we can be as free as we want, without limits. Such a realization is so radical that it can be realized only gradually. A famous guru was once asked if enlightenment could be achieved quickly. He replied, "It can happen in thirty days, but you would need thirty men to hold you down."

It's impossible to quantify if you are on the spiritual path or how far along it you may be. But progress is always marked by transformation. The path isn't about feeling better. It's not about knowing who you are, or ending your suffering, or finding peace, or healing your deepest wounds. It's about a transformation so profound that illusion is traded for reality. Jesus survives to this day as a force in the world because he embodied that truth completely. As we are heading for God-consciousness, our own transformation cannot stop halfway; we can't settle for a better life or even the best life, for a glimpse of God, or even for God as a daily companion. The state of God-consciousness represents a leap in human development that you and I must be prepared to make personally. The middle of the path brings us to the leaping-off point. The end of the journey will look nothing like the world we took our leap from.

WHERE THE SOUL NEVER DIES

※

What will it feel like to finally arrive in God-consciousness? Anyone traveling the spiritual path will naturally ask this question. The middle of the journey isn't the same as the destination. The mixture of old and new self must eventually resolve into a completely new self. Sin will no longer exist. God's grace will be abundant, and his presence will guide our every action. That, at least, is the promise that sets people on the spiritual path to begin with if their goal is God-consciousness. When God-consciousness dawns, a complex series of changes occurs:

> There is no longer a battle between good and evil.
> Fear is revealed as an illusion.
> You identify with God—your thoughts and desires
> have a divine source.
> You feel that the world is yours as co-creator with God.
> The world "out there" responds immediately to the world
> "in here"—in other words, outward reality mirrors the self.
> Love is realized as the supreme force in the universe.

These qualities have been developing over time, first appearing as scattered experiences and flashes of the truth, then becoming more frequent. Imagine a lab study in which a person's awareness is being monitored around the clock, with researchers asking him to push a red button when he feels the presence of God. In an ordinary waking state the button might never be pressed. This first subject isn't aware of God, or if he feels something different that might be God, he has no word for it, no sense that it may be connected to a higher source. When a second subject feels particularly joyful, she attributes that feeling to God and presses the button.

The researchers move on to a new subject, a woman who has been on the spiritual path for some time. She presses the red button more often. One can think of two reasons why. First, she has learned to identify an inner state with God; second, she has expectations that this state will return. Why? Because her mind has learned to notice things that people ordinarily don't, and when she does, she can put a word—God—to such feelings. We have to be vague here, because there's an enormous amount of variation. For some people on the path, God's presence means inner peace and tranquillity, while for others, it means the opposite, a sudden influx of rapture that heightens all sensations, making them unusually vivid.

Our researchers are open-minded; they can accept the fact that there might be as many kinds of experiences as there are people. Instead of defining God in advance, they let their subjects define him (keeping in mind that "him" itself is just a conventional term, not a quality of God, who is beyond gender). Now they turn to people who consider themselves very near to God. They don't have to be monks or nuns or priests. They could come from any walk of life, but they do have one thing in common: They seem to find God in many things, so many that they press the red button quite frequently.

Eventually, if you sort through enough subjects, you will find someone who keeps his finger on the button all the time. This person is in God-consciousness. There are no gaps in his experience between when God is present and when he is not. For this subject God is a steady reality, like breathing or being awake. What creates such a person? Here we can't afford to be vague, because a radical change has occurred that must be understood correctly. It's not enough to press the red button every ten minutes, or even every ten seconds, to be in God-consciousness. As long as the mind is dipping in and out of ordinary experience, the ego retains a foothold.

God and ego aren't compatible. At first they seem to be. We all differentiate two sides of our nature. One side is the self devoted to the outer world and all its demands; the other is the inner, private self. The ego attempts to control both sides of this divide, but this is an illusion. In the outer world, the ego can create all kinds of situations where "I" has a stake in the outcome. Whole departments of life, including job, relationships, and social status, belong in the ego's domain.

But more is going on inside than a mirror reflection of the ego's world. We are aware of beauty and truth. We feel led by intuitions and insights. In scattered moments we sense something beyond. None of these experiences is ego created. In fact, they are its enemy. Anything that gives a hint of life's wholeness, any experience that transcends "I, me, and mine," threatens the ego's claim to dominance. This is because by definition, "I" is a separate entity. It wants certain things and not others. It wants to make friends out of some egos and enemies out of others. The one thing it can't abide is the reality that separate egos don't exist, that everything comes from a single source. Jesus brought just such a message to earth, and although he labeled it "God," in keeping with the language of his time, words aren't the same as experience.

Christianity has focused for centuries on the reaction that Jesus's message created. Anyone raised in the faith has felt Jesus's pain as he met with constant misunderstanding, rejection, and persecution. It was all he could do to survive, and he didn't do that for long. But to focus on the reaction to Jesus misses the point; it turns the Jesus story into another ego battle—his against that of everyone else (less a handful of disciples, who grasped the truth). Our focus should be on Jesus's truth, which transcends its reception in the material world. In other faiths, such as Buddhism, there was just as much misunderstanding, but the ground was more fertile. Buddha wasn't met with persecution; the people he mystified revered him anyway.

We can't change Christian history, but we can understand it better by setting aside the persecution. It belongs to the ego's world, where the battle between light and dark is an eternal drama. Jesus fell into the drama by becoming a public figure, but he wasn't part of it personally. The same holds true for anyone who reaches God-consciousness. At a certain point, wholeness prevails. There is no more going in and out of God, coming to God and moving away. The experience of God turns into a constant for one reason alone: "I" and "God" become one and the same. The truth that Jesus spoke wasn't a collection of insights, or messages from God. His words were the product of his state of mind. We must be very clear on that point, because God-consciousness cannot be reduced to psychology. It's not like feeling young or knowing that your spouse loves you. If I sense the presence of God, then in some way I have entered God's identity and taken it as my own. Were it not for this quality of union, Jesus's message would not be radical. He would just be one among many people who love God and feel close to him.

To be completely reliable, a state of higher awareness needs to be as different from everyday awareness as sleeping is from dreaming. Touchy issues arise here. If someone claims to feel the presence of God, is there a test we can apply to find out if he's telling the truth? Pontius Pilate might have freed Jesus if he'd had the benefit of a lie detector. On the other hand, he may have decided that a man who is hallucinating about God isn't lying; he's just deluded. God-consciousness resists being verified because it bridges two worlds. In the material world a person may look unchanged (barring some kind of brain scan that can detect enlightenment), but if you put the red button in his hand, he won't be able to register a moment when God is absent. This is the exact opposite of our ordinary waking state. To close that gap once and for all, you yourself must be in God-consciousness.

The New Testament offers Jesus himself as the example of what a totally transformed person would be like. But Jesus is the very thing you and I *won't* be like once we arrive at God-consciousness. Every life is different, and many of those differences are dictated by history. The arrival of Jesus in the first century AD was entangled with the Roman persecution of the Jews. His story would be shaped by the destruction of the Second Temple in 70 AD, which crushed the Jewish people and their hope of divine rescue. The four gospels were written after that catastrophic event, and there's no doubt that the writers were holding out Jesus and his promises as the best new hope for the future.

None of those factors is relevant today. We retain the same words—sin, redemption, salvation, Messiah—like worn coins. But sin today occurs in a wildly changed context and a more confusing one. Is sin the same as a crime, mental illness, defective ego development, Karma, nature, or poor genetic programming? Is redemption a subjective state that makes you feel better, free of neurosis, and capable of fulfilling your potential? Or is it still an escape from the fiery pit of Hell? It's not accurate to assume that our spiritual needs are identical to those of someone in the distant past, however much the old words from their story resonate in our heads.

Meaning Moves On

Every religion runs into the same historical problem. If we turn to the life of Buddha, who spoke in universal terms about enlightenment, we find that his followers were illiterate, mostly impoverished

Indians of the fifth century BC. They toiled the land from birth, died young, and suffered many travails along the way. They had no power over who governed them, politically or spiritually. Just as the Jews of Jesus's time had their entire lives prescribed by hundreds of duties enforced by the priesthood, so did the Hindus of Buddha's time. All of this shaped their spiritual path, so we can't automatically translate the vision that Buddha offered them into our day.

One thing that God-consciousness will bring back, however, is the magic of discovery. There are no dark places left on the map anymore, but if there were, I imagine that Christian missionaries could penetrate a hidden rain forest somewhere on the globe and astonish the native people with the story of Jesus. I imagine them listening wide-eyed (as we once did in childhood) to the tale of the man who walked on water and rose from the dead, who could heal with a touch, and who spoke directly to God. Evoking the same wonder in latter-day Christians, whose cultures were converted centuries ago, grows ever more difficult. Happily, God-consciousness is a miraculous state on its own. It's the leap in evolution that Jesus promised to his followers, something far better than listening to his miracle story generation after generation.

"I haven't gone to church in years," a friend told me recently. "But nostalgia tugged at me, so this Christmas I drove alone to midnight Mass. This particular church is attached to a monastery, and when I walked in, the air was smoky with incense. The monks formed a robed procession, a boys choir sang invisibly over our heads. The whole space was glowing in soft, amber candlelight. There was even a bishop holding his shepherd's crook at the door to thank us for coming. I felt like I had stepped into a medieval painting.

"I fell into a mood that's hard to describe. The ceremony was uplifting, and part of me couldn't resist that, but I'm divorced, and my credit cards are maxed out. I've never had a prayer answered when I needed it most. I'm disgusted by fundamentalism, and yet disgusted with myself for having no belief anymore. I felt a terrible longing and deep sadness at the same time just shreds of memory."

The beautiful moods that Christianity arouses are powerful but temporary, and they stem almost entirely from the life story of Jesus. A great deal of what he actually said doesn't apply anymore. Jesus told his listeners that he had come to fulfill a prophecy with which they were intensely familiar. A messiah would bring about the rulership of God on earth, and at the same time the Bible would come full circle. Paradise would be regained, and Jesus would lead a race of new Adams and Eves back into Eden.

That's exactly what happened to at least one follower we know of, Saint Paul, who spread the news of "a new Heaven and a new earth" everywhere he traveled, through Palestine, Syria, and beyond. His conversion experience was spectacular. From a worldly skeptic who persecuted the early Christians, he became a fiery believer. The traditional story is that a light blinded him as he rode to Damascus, and Jesus's voice said, "Why do you persecute me?" We don't get that story from Paul himself, however, so it may be dramatically exaggerated. But the explosion of spirit in Paul's life isn't. What he experienced became the model for future generations seeking salvation: In a flash a sinner sees the light and recognizes God. It also filled a void, for as much as the gospels tell us about Jesus, they have almost nothing to say about *his* path to God. Jesus isn't converted in the New Testament, because he had no sins to redeem. If he went through a process of discovering that he was the Messiah, the gospel writers do not record it; Jesus himself makes no references to finding God.

According to the chronology we have, Jesus is born, he goes to Jerusalem with his parents when he's twelve, and then he emerges to be baptized by John the Baptist when he is around thirty. The episode that occurs at age twelve occurs only in the gospel of Luke, and it is highly symbolic. Mary and Joseph travel to Jerusalem, as they did every year, for the feast of Passover. They would have been obliged to do this by law and custom (strangely, Jesus himself seems to have entered Jerusalem only once as an adult, in violation of both law and custom). At the end of Passover his parents begin their journey home to Nazareth, only to discover that Jesus isn't with their group anymore but has stayed behind in Jerusalem without their knowledge. They turn back and anxiously search for him. Three days later they locate their son listening to priests and teachers in the temple.

So far, the most obvious symbolic element is the three-day search, which prefigures the three days before Christ's resurrection from the dead, although at a deeper level the story is the same—Jesus disappears and is found again. When his parents see him among the priests and teachers, Jesus "was listening to them and asking them questions. And all who heard him were amazed at his understanding and his answers." (Luke 2:46–47) His mother rebukes the boy for abandoning them: "Child, why have you treated us like this? Look, your father and I have been searching for you in great anxiety." He said to them, "Why were you searching for me? Did you not know that I must be in my Father's house?" (Luke 2:48–50)

Already we are hearing the voice of the adult Jesus, supremely confident in his identity. Mary and Joseph, however, were still seeing him through their role as parents. But they did not understand what he said to them. Then he went down with them and came to Nazareth, and was obedient to them. His mother treasured all these things in her heart. (Luke 2:50–51)

The gospel writer has given us another aspect of the adult Jesus, his meekness. But then the Messiah's biography becomes obscure. We learn nothing except for a hint, in the next verse: "And Jesus increased in wisdom and in years, and in divine and human favor." The implication is that despite his precocious wisdom, the young Jesus was capable of more growth. This implies that he walked a path, but of what sort we have no idea. By comparison, Buddha's path from coddled prince to the Compassionate One is full of human details (most of them culled from legends, myths, and local tales hundreds of years after the fact).

The Rescue Is Unity

History may blur Jesus's biography, but it can't put out the light. The rescue that was promised to the Jews of the first century has a universal aspect. We may not be waiting to be rescued from Roman persecution, yet in our way we are waiting to be saved. The gospels tell a truth that people still want to hear, because certain conditions never change. People still suffer and feel abandoned. They continue to yearn for a transcendent reality. Above all, the condition of separation hasn't been addressed. All the troubles that stem from the ego and its desperate isolation continue to weigh down individual existence. The rescue that people need today won't conquer Caesar, but it will conquer duality. Jesus symbolized the transcendent self that renders the ego irrelevant and transforms duality into oneness with God.

Unity remains mysterious to this day, and many people who are on the spiritual path can't envision it. They imagine that the goal of seeking is greater happiness, peace of mind, and wisdom. Jesus holds out a genuine vision of the goal. "Unity" is just an abstract concept until we connect with his description of the actual experience; here, in brief, are the best clues we have from Jesus himself.

Jesus saw himself as beyond death. "And remember, I am with you always, to the end of the age." (Matthew 28:20)

He considered his teachings to transcend history, even time itself. "Heaven and earth will pass away, but my words will not pass away." (Matthew 24:35)

He enclosed everyone in his being. "You have already been cleansed by the word that I have spoken to you. Abide in me as I abide in you." (John 15:3–4)

He regarded unity as the only way to escape death and destruction. ". . . apart from me you can do nothing. Whoever does not abide in me is thrown away like a branch and withers; such branches are gathered, thrown into the fire, and burned." (John 15:5–6)

He felt the sensation of love as divine. "As the Father has loved me, so I have loved you; abide in my love." (John 15:9)

All spiritual questioning ended with him. "All authority in heaven and on earth has been given to me." (Matthew 28:18)

Traditionally, these passages (and dozens like them) testify to Jesus's conviction that he was the Messiah, but we can read them in a different way, as the natural expression of a man in unity. Jesus doesn't tell us how he arrived at unity, so we have no before and after to compare. (Buddha, on the other hand, does provide us with a dramatic story of his life as a prince and warrior before he attained enlightenment, yet like Jesus, he hardly ever made personal references to himself once he had reached unity.)

Certain qualities of unity emerge very clearly. Unity is

impersonal
powerful
deathless
all-knowing
creative
loving

The four gospels may confuse us on many points, but not these. In Jesus we see a person for whom the small "I" has merged with the universal "I," whose behavior reflects that shift.

This is also the reason why Jesus proves so elusive, for unity has no qualities that can be brought down-to-earth and made human. Christianity has done everything possible to humanize Jesus, for we cannot conceive of someone so completely transcendent that even our most cherished qualities, such as love and compassion, fall short of his reality. In India the tradition of unity is older and more sea-soned; there is less panic about not appealing to the crowd. In that context, unity is described in less human terms, as

unborn
undying
unbounded
unlimited
inexpressible
ineffable
unknowable to the mind and the five senses

Now we are erasing everything that we identify with as human beings. You and I accept that we were born and will die. A person in unity thinks we've been fooled by appearances, that only the physi-cal body is born and dies. You and I feel limited in what we can do; we value our ability to express who we are and how we feel; we stay within certain boundaries and are afraid to venture beyond them. All of this strikes someone in unity as pure illusion.

If Jesus was in unity—as he declared over and over—then we must accept that his experience can't be grasped by expanding our own. That's always a temptation. I love my children, Jesus says that he loves me, therefore Jesus loves me as I love my children. No, in this case, the equation breaks down. Jesus loves me in a way I cannot fathom until I reach unity myself. He invites me to walk the spiri-tual path in order to find something beyond words, beyond even his own. Unity is the fate that releases the grip of fate, the destiny that obliterates all that came before or will come after. No matter how many ways it gets reworded, unity can't be compared to anything but itself. The miracle, and the joy, is how beautiful Jesus made the goal appear, even to a blind humanity.

WHAT WOULD JESUS DO?

*

I could not conclude a book about Jesus without delving into the social crisis that Christianity currently faces. Not just in America but around the world, the faith has been hijacked by movements that violate Jesus's teaching even as they proclaim they are defending it. A religion of love has moved alarmingly in the direction of hatred, although outright hatred may not be preached from the pulpit. What is preached is self-righteous intolerance.

Recently I saw a television news feature on a new movement in education, Christian law schools. Not satisfied with two hundred years of separation between church and state, or the simple fact that the Constitution never once mentions God, fundamentalists are taking a new tack. They are teaching students that criminal and civil law is rooted in God's commandments. In the news feature a recent graduate of one of these Christian law schools was interviewed on camera, a beaming young woman who said, "We're not out to indoctrinate anybody, but to share the truth, and to rely on the truth in the way we handle our own lives." With her gentle, reasonable manner, she was the opposite of the stereotype of intolerance. But as easily as the word *truth* spilled from her lips, one sensed something disturbing. She went on to say, "I believe in absolute truth. Not in gray or relative truth. Absolute truth is where God's word is." Her affable, reasonable manner didn't change, and yet she had stepped unwittingly into the danger zone of zealotry. It was graduation day at her Christian law school in Virginia, which has sent more than a hundred alumni into the highest ranks of the federal bureaucracy, thanks to a fervent fundamentalist who serves as hiring officer for the executive branch in Washington.

Other new graduates spoke confidently of "God's word" being the ultimate basis of the law in all times and places. This cadre of young Christian lawyers is ambitious, intent on overturning gay rights and legal abortion, reaching into stem cell research, school prayer, and beyond. Has anyone told them that God's word (that is, the Bible) is explicitly out of bounds in a secular state, or that God has faces other than Christian? They have been betrayed by elders who assure them that "God's word" endorses reactionary politics.

When we read headlines about gay bashing and violent attacks on abortion clinics, the media are careful not to draw a direct line to fundamentalist dogma, but that is a mere formality. Society has been led by "two sides to every story" into believing that intolerance is the other side of an ongoing social debate, and perhaps the more virtuous. Fundamentalist Christians, after all, proclaim their devotion to life, family values, and regular religious observance.

This trend may eventually cripple Christianity. In every denomination reactionary and progressive forces struggle for power, and one would be hard-pressed to find a case where the reactionaries aren't winning. They equate taking the Bible literally with being a good Christian, despite the mountain of evidence—only a fraction of it mentioned in this book—that Jesus's teachings have been muddled, obscured, altered, corrupted, and lost over the centuries. Attempts to return to the pure origin of Christianity are doomed from the start, but this only fuels fundamentalist zeal.

The tragic irony behind this crisis is revealed by a favorite fundamentalist slogan: "What would Jesus do?" It has become familiar on bumper stickers and in presidential races. The novelty of the slogan has worn off, yet countless Christians (and not just fundamentalists) use "What would Jesus do?" as their moral touchstone. Without being conscious of it, perhaps, they have fallen back on the medieval tradition of *Imitatio Christi*, worshipping Christ by imitating him.

Why is this worrisome? On the face of it, the image of Jesus as kind, compassionate, loving, and forgiving seems like an impeccable model of morality. But as we have seen, Jesus doesn't fit that simplistic image. Nor can we extrapolate from the words found in the gospels. On the most hotly debated social issues that now split Christianity, the gospels provide no clear resolution. In fact, the bitter conflict over such issues as gay rights and abortion is only made worse by referring these tough moral choices to Jesus. If anyone is serious about asking "What would Jesus do?" the first question to ask is, "What would Jesus do about the mess that Christianity finds itself in?"

Abortion—The abortion debate straddles two worlds, the secular and the religious. Most of us feel that we have a foot in both, which muddies the abortion issue from the very outset. Two different languages are being spoken, and no translation encompasses both. In secular terms, terminating a pregnancy is a medical procedure, and the decision is made for personal or biological reasons. As a matter of law, the woman in question has rights over what happens to her own body. The unborn fetus represents a primitive form of human life, little more than a clumped mass of cells if termination is sought early enough. In terms of morality, the secular position is that the woman and her immediate family, along with the man in question, should make their decision privately. Some would go so far as to make the choice entirely private, belonging to the woman and no one else.

In religious terms, none of these arguments are convincing to conservative Christians. For centuries the Catholic Church has considered a fetus sacred from the moment of conception. Fundamentalism has adopted that position but did not invent it. The two sects make strange allies. In the case of fundamentalism, scripture is the source of all truth, because only scripture is authentically divine. On the other hand, the Catholic Church has been adding to scripture since the beginning, and the literal meaning of the New Testament forms only the core of belief. A host of saints, church councils, learned theologians, and popes have altered Jesus's teachings while adopting his authority. On the face of it, then, there should be strong antagonism between Catholics and fundamentalists. To come together over abortion, a long rancorous rivalry had to be overlooked.

To claim that Jesus would condemn abortion means that one has chosen a very specific Jesus, the orthodox rabbi who cautions his followers that they must obey the laws of Moses. Such a Jesus certainly exists, and since the Old Testament condemns abortion, this allows pro-lifers to skirt one significant problem: Jesus himself does not mention abortion. For that matter, he doesn't touch on the other critical questions in the abortion debate, such as when the soul enters an infant, how to balance the health of the mother with the survival of a fetus, and who has rights over a woman's body. In the total disconnect between secular and religious language, Jesus doesn't help at all.

Because there is more than one Jesus, the one who strictly obeys the laws of Moses isn't the one who forgives and shows tolerance. Nor is he the Jesus who rebukes the Pharisees for obeying the letter of the law and ignoring its spirit. That Jesus is being ignored by fundamentalists. If they prefer the strict Jesus, then what about his absolute injunction against divorce? There is also the mystical Jesus to consider, who saw the material world as an illusion and explicitly denied that he had come to settle worldly affairs. When he told Pilate that his kingdom was not on earth, Jesus made a blanket statement. By no means does Jesus provide support for the anti-abortion cause unless we accept Church doctrine as speaking for him.

Gay rights—There is a long tradition of condemning homosexuality in Judeo-Christianity. Again, this stricture was transferred from the Old Testament, since Jesus himself is silent on this issue. It isn't possible to limit Jesus to the conventions of his time. For all that he respects those mores, he also criticizes them. The parable of the Good Samaritan seems particularly relevant here: A man lies injured in a ditch, and all the righteous people on the road ignore him, while only a Samaritan, coming from a despised class, offers help. If fundamentalists want to take their cue from Jesus, this teaching demonstrates that he was on the side of the despised.

A friend recently told me about an encounter he'd had with an Episcopal priest. "This was several years ago, when the Episcopalians voted to allow a gay man to become a bishop. I raised the topic with a local priest and asked him how he had voted. 'Against,' he said sternly. I asked him why. 'Because a gay lifestyle is against God's wishes,' he said without hesitation.

"I asked him how he knew which lifestyle was against God's wishes, given that homosexuality isn't mentioned by Jesus. 'We have the Old Testament,' he said, 'and besides, one just knows.'

"I'm not a committed Christian, but his self-assurance amazed me. 'What about polygamy?' I said. 'And the practice of a man divorcing a wife by rejecting her and throwing her out? Not to mention the total subjugation of women. Those exist in the Old Testament, don't they?'

"He looked completely unperturbed. 'Times change,' he murmured.

"'Exactly,' I shot back."

My friend was taking the rationalist position. Customs change with time, so it isn't fair to permit change only when you happen to approve of it but condemn change citing biblical authority when you don't. This is the very hypocrisy that Jesus accuses the priests of—that is, tailoring the law to fit their prejudices. Can we go further and claim that Jesus would not have seen homosexuality as a sin? The point is moot, because Jesus came into the world to forgive all sins. At the Last Supper he explicitly states that his blood is being spilled as a sign of a new covenant between man and God, and that this new agreement is the forgiveness of sin. We don't need anyone's guess that Jesus might or might not have condemned homosexuality. We know that the thieves on either side of the cross were grave sinners, and yet Jesus offered them entry into the Kingdom of God without condemnation or approval. There is no litmus test for deserving God's grace.

Women's rights—For many Christian conservatives, women are second-class members of the church, if not worse. Episcopalians are bitterly divided not just over gays, but over the right of women to serve as priests. The Catholic Church shows no sign of budging on the rule that priests be male, unmarried, and celibate. This despite the fact that for the first six centuries after Christ's death, there was no requirement for priests to be celibate, and in many Gnostic sects women were given equal status with men in church services, where direct inspiration was spontaneously received by anyone in the congregation.

Jesus did not live at a time of women's issues as we define them. His most famous act toward a woman was to forgive the sins of "the woman taken in adultery," as she is called in English. This incident, which appears in the Gospel of John, may refer to Mary Magdalene, but that is a matter of conjecture. The Gnostic Gospels that came to light in the late Forties but were not widely disseminated until thirty years later shocked devout Christians with passages where Mary Magdalene becomes a prominent disciple. Jesus takes her side in a dispute with Simon Peter and goes so far as to condemn Peter for his attitude against women.

Raising Mary Magdalene to favored status among the disciples dramatically reverses Christian tradition, but it also exposes the losing battle that forgiveness has waged in the Church. Women have borne the brunt of the sins of Eve since the earliest days of Judaism. (Some biblical scholars trace this back to early migrations, when the Jews came into contact with other civilizations that worshipped a female goddess. They wanted to differentiate themselves from goddess worship in the most decisive way, and making a woman the source of evil in the world certainly accomplished that.) The story of Eve fixed in place a belief system that lingered into the Christian era. Women were weak, given to temptation. Their sexual allure was a moral failing that placed them against God.

The early Christians declared Christ the New Adam, but they clung fiercely to the old Eve. Social mores proved stronger than the Messiah, and therefore by the time of Paul, which was only a few decades after the Crucifixion, we find little or no effort to forgive women their inherent sinfulness. Rather, Paul adopts it as part of the Church's official value system.

To counter Eve's image, the ideal of Mary arose. In the Hail Mary, the phrase *full of grace* refers to a church doctrine that exempted her from original sin. Yet even Mary was not totally exempt from suspicion. The Church recognized the Feast of the

Immaculate Conception in the fifteenth century but made clear that Catholics could choose personally whether to believe in Mary's total purity. Not until 1854 would a pope officially make the Immaculate Conception sacred dogma. (To clarify an often confused point, the Immaculate Conception isn't the same as the virgin birth. The first refers to Mary being born completely without sin, the second to Christ being conceived without sexual union.)

Christian women often find themselves caught between Eve and Mary, either vilified or idealized. That leaves not much middle ground. Yet rationally, women are not the daughters of Eve; their sexuality isn't sinful; their proximity to God is the same as a man's. To someone outside the faith, these points are self-evident. But religion depends on a worldview that isn't fully consistent with reason. The miracle world of Jesus wasn't reasonable, and a devout believer in that world becomes immune to arguments from a secular worldview. Eve and Mary may be diametrically opposed, yet the legacy of both is supernatural. Without a woman, evil would not have entered the world, but neither would miraculous salvation. Woman is capable of utmost sin and utmost purity.

This is one area where fundamentalists stand ahead of many other Christians. Being a Protestant movement, fundamentalism has abandoned the doctrine of intercession through the Virgin Mary and has little or no cult of sainthood. Women preach freely in many sects, and the Pentecostal tradition allows anyone of either sex to speak in tongues, a legacy that can be traced back to the Gnostics. It's ironic that the most reactionary wing of Christianity has proved the most progressive with regard to women.

War—Mixing patriotism with religion has always been lethal yet all too common. Jesus is a most unlikely figure to justify a war. The word *peace* appears 344 times in the Bible, and for a strife-torn people like the Jews, whose history was inseparably bound up with violence against them, the Messiah was above all a peacemaker. By contrast, although the Bible uses the word *war* 231 times (not counting synonyms like *battle* and *strife*), it is not used once in the four gospels. ("War" crops up most prominently in the Book of Revelation, which describes the apocalyptic war between good and evil that draws in the Four Horsemen, Satan, the archangel Michael, the hosts of angels and demons, and Christ himself.)

Foretelling the Messiah, the prophet Isaiah declares, "His authority shall grow continually, and there shall be endless peace for the throne of David and his kingdom." (Isaiah 9:7) God is beseeched for peace constantly in the Psalms, and although political peace is the primary focus, personal and universal peace have their place as well. When Jesus came to bring peace, his mission began with the Jews but was intended as peace for everyone.

The first time that Jesus refers to peace is in Matthew's account of the Sermon on the Mount. "Blessed are the peacemakers, for they will be called children of God." (Matthew 5:9) In the next book of this gospel Jesus makes an inflammatory and self-contradictory statement: "Do not think that I have come to bring peace to the earth; I have not come to bring peace but a sword." (Matthew 10:34) The statement is mystifying in light of the many other times that Jesus calls himself a peacemaker. Some clarity might come from his references to the turmoil that is brought into people's lives when they are exposed to divine truth. Symbolically, the sword that Jesus brings may be the kind that upsets and transforms people's lives inside. Or we may simply have lost the actual context that Jesus was speaking in.

Everyone, not just fundamentalists, can fall into an easy assumption that Jesus would be in favor of a "good war," one that God approves of. Scripture contradicts this assumption. War is absent, peace is constantly emphasized. "Go in peace" and "Be at peace" are typical phrases from Jesus. Of the twenty-three times he uses the word *peace* in the four gospels, about half are in this form. The angels declared peace on earth and goodwill among men the moment that Jesus was born. The concept appears foremost in his teachings, along with love, as Jesus makes clear in the simplest ways. He instructs his disciples, "Whatever house you enter, first say, 'Peace to this house.'" (Luke 10:5) In the current political climate in the United States, God is invoked regularly by the religious right to justify war against Islamic terrorism. The notion that God favors war derives from the belligerence of Jehovah in the Old Testament, and yet I find it significant how little Jesus himself is invoked in the fight against al-Qaeda. The Messiah's dedication to peace is embarrassing to modern Christianity, perhaps, so he is shunted aside in favor of invoking God.

My thoughts drift back to the smiling young woman graduating from a Christian law school. At one point she said, "I believe in absolute truth. Not in gray or relative truth. Absolute truth is where God's word is." Does she see how closely she echoes the ideology of the jihadis, for whom truth is so absolute and God-given that they gladly strap themselves to suicide bombs? The great danger of invoking the deity when you go off to war is that the other side is doing the same thing. Once war becomes a clash of absolutes, there is no breathing room for mercy. Absolute truth is blind truth. When rival ideologies clash over which one owns the truth, they fall into the same trap: Wars waged in the name of God wander as far from that truth as anyone can conceive. The hellish condition of war cannot be justified in spiritual terms.

Let's be candid here. The readers of this book are very unlikely to be Christian fundamentalists. The shortcomings of the religious right have been widely aired, also, so why repeat them one more time? Because the crisis in Christianity is a challenge to action. Twenty-five years ago, few observers predicted that reactionary religious forces could become as vociferous and powerful as they are today. Social divisions are more bitter than ever. Actually applying Jesus's message couldn't come at a more important time.

What would Jesus do? I have no doubt that he wouldn't refer moral issues to a fixed code or to Church authority; he wouldn't bow to social pressure; he wouldn't be quick to raise himself above those who are labeled sinners. People who do any of those things aren't spiritually motivated. They are falling back upon the lowest aspect of human nature, the tendency to condemn and punish anyone who is different. You and I can't change the behavior of the religious right, but the passive reaction of many moderate and liberal Christians, which causes them to suffer in silence or walk away, is self-defeating.

Personal growth is achieved by acting according to your own spiritual vision. If Jesus is your model of spiritual greatness, his tenets lead to action.

Courage—Jesus was brave in the face of overwhelming odds. He took for granted that if he stood up to wrongdoing, he drew close to God. Jesus spans more than one archetype, but in his courage he stands for the hero. The hero begins as one man against the world, but he ends by representing a new world. The enemy of courage is fear, which wears many masks. You can fear being different, or failure, or humiliation, or ostracism. Yet these are only reflections of a single condition: living behind boundaries. Bigots may seem brave, yet because their fight is always to build the walls and shut others out, intolerant people are acting from fear. When you realize that, the spiritual path opens up. You find that a single goal—overcoming fear—is the primary purpose of any quest. Courage renews the self by breaking boundaries.

Truth-telling—Because the truth sets people free, Jesus used the truth as an agent of change. When you tell the truth, you speak to the truth in others. They may hide from their own truth, but you are seeking to free them, and in the process you make your truth stronger. The crucial words here are "your truth," which is personal, relative, and never the same as God's absolute truth. But to call the truth relative isn't the same as calling it weak. Relative refers to the fact that we each have a personal perspective and cannot see through anyone else's eyes.

Sympathy and tolerance—In a divided society there are many reasons not to offer sympathy to others. They are familiar enough to all of us. We feel safe with our own kind, like-minded people who reassure us that "we" are right and "they" are wrong. It becomes hard to see the truth, which is not that you and your kind are right. You just happen to agree. Imagine the people whose values are dead set against yours, and know that they and their kind feel just as right as you do.

It's difficult to let this truth sink in, but nothing is more important. Two contending sides are equal at the level where "I am right and you are wrong" exists. This ego-driven voice is an enemy to spiritual growth. The ego refuses to give up its certainty, isolation, competition, and antagonism. Jesus saw the problem clearly, and his answer—one of the most consistent answers he ever gave—was to see the world from the viewpoint of the humblest, weakest, and poorest.

Jesus taught humility not just as an antidote to pride but as another way to become free. The ego, with all its wishes, fears, ambitions, likes, and dislikes, dominates everyone's existence, and therefore almost no one sees the truth, which is that the ego is an enormous burden. Its concerns are endless, its anxieties inescapable. Its victories are temporary, and its isolation is crippling. To get his followers to see this truth clearly, Jesus wanted them to experience what it is like to be powerless, overlooked, and unknown. In other words, to be last. The ego cannot tolerate being last, since its insatiable goal is to be first.

As of this writing, religious fundamentalists are riding high politically; although a minority in society, the religious right has pursued power with dedication and discipline. The fundamentalist mind-set sees its adherents as outsiders, the downtrodden and misunderstood. In a sense far removed from Jesus's meaning, the last have become first. Can you and I sympathize? Of course we can; everyone has experienced enough rejection and failure to know how it feels to be last. The point isn't to judge the religious right. Not only would such behavior not be enlightened, it would be totally counterproductive as a strategy. The motto fundamentalists march under is, "As long as you hate us, we aren't going away."

Will sympathy make them go away? No, but it will soften and in time dissolve their embattled rigidity. Nothing brings down walls as surely as acceptance. By embracing the poor and weak, Jesus redeemed them in their own eyes. He added to their lives the one thing they couldn't create on their own: a sense of worth. At every stage of our spiritual growth, each of us can give the same gift. We can see more worth in others than they see in themselves.

Love and forgiveness—In the current crisis, these words have taken on a bitter taste. The religious right congratulates itself for spreading Jesus's message of love, while at the same time practicing social condemnation and exclusion. This is the deepest irony, made more bitter by the futility of using love to change such intolerance. What good does it do to tolerate the intolerant? When fundamentalists began their incursions into the contented, sleepy precincts of Lutherans, Methodists, and Episcopalians, they were met with polite dismay. When they kept pushing, making it clear that gays, ordained women, and abortion were intolerable to "good Christians," dismay turned to confusion. Moderate Christians tried to seek common ground, to find moderate compromises, but such tactics are fruitless when the person on the other side of the negotiating table is absolutely immovable.

What, then, to do? The paradox of Christian love isn't new, and the church has failed at "Love thy enemy" over and over. This failure has encouraged it not to speak out against war, intolerance, and social stigmatism of minorities. You and I are left to solve the problem on our own, since no higher authority is going to do it for us. The challenge isn't easy. Nor does it lead to a single answer. Rather, you must trust in your ability to love as you grow spiritually. In higher states of consciousness, love has power. Change that is rooted in nonlove doesn't actually solve anything. Two people who hate each other's opinions are mirrors of the same dilemma; it doesn't matter if one is a fundamentalist and the other a liberal. Love is many things, but two stand out in particular: It's the truth, and it's an experience. Jesus said that by experiencing the truth of love, you grow beyond nonlove and nontruth.

In the early part of the twenty-first century, there is more than enough nonlove and nontruth for everyone to claim a portion. You and I know whom we don't really forgive and whom we pretend to tolerate. We know what it's like to wear a mask for social reasons that have little to do with our deepest feelings. Moving out of that predicament is what spirituality is about. The soul loves and forgives automatically; it sees beyond all divisions, however deep; it wears no masks. And the soul isn't a distant goal but a hidden aspect of the self. In the end, all crises are passing affairs. The particulars of abortion seem extremely important right now; the particulars of whether unbaptized infants went to Hell were of equal importance three or four centuries ago.

Jesus taught that this moment is ephemeral. Today's winner will lose tomorrow, and vice versa. The space cleared by one solved problem will be instantly filled by a new problem dilemma. In a world where winning and losing are two sides of the same illusion, there is a third way. Use today's crisis for tomorrow's growth. It's Christian to engage with love. When you don't engage, you cannot experience your authenticity. You cannot prove your degree of love, tolerance, and forgiveness against your hidden prejudice, intolerance, and judgment. External conflicts serve that purpose—and that purpose alone—on the spiritual path. They reflect the internal state of conflict that needs to be healed, and in this way you discover how much distance separates you from your soul.

Now we can view the schism in Christianity not as another wearisome political battle, or a contest between right and wrong. Rather, this is a drama being projected from the inner world to the outer. You and I are drawn into the drama because it's our drama. We were meant to engage with it as part of our spiritual contract. The oppressor and the victim, the wrongdoer and the wronged, the weak and the powerful, all exist in me. I can't resolve every division, but at the soul level I've resolved the ones I need to advance my journey for now. What would Jesus do in my shoes? He would keep walking the path. He would manifest as much courage, truth, sympathy, and love as he actually possessed. He wouldn't pretend to be what he wasn't. The Son of Man was most human when he mirrored the conflicts of everyday life, a plane of existence that he knew intimately even as he rose above it. Your goal and mine isn't to imitate Jesus. It is to become part of him—or, as he said, to abide in him. We can do that at the level of consciousness by becoming part of the unending process that turns separation into unity. Our lives belong to that process as surely as the life of the Messiah did.

INDEX

ABOUT THE AUTHOR

✦

DEEPAK CHOPRA is the author of more than fifty books translated in over thirty-five languages, including numerous *New York Times* best-sellers in both the fiction and nonfiction categories. Chopra's Wellness Radio airs weekly on Sirius Satellite Stars, Channel 102, which focuses on the areas of success, love, sexuality and relationships, well-being, and spirituality. He is founder and president of the Alliance for a New Humanity. *Time* magazine heralds Deepak Chopra as one of the top one hundred heroes and icons of the century, and credits him as "the poet-prophet of alternative medicine."

www.deepakchopra.com